contents

editorial

new poetry

fiction

essays and interviews

learning curve

reviews

recommendations

reading lives

the back end

Starting in this issue, we will be scattering quotations from one or two great works throughout the magazine. The featured books in issue 20 are Edward Thomas, *Collected Poems* and Bernard Malamud, *Dubin's Lives*.

Smash the Nature Table

Jane Davis

D.H. Lawrence thought the word 'love' ought to be erased from the language for a time so that we could start to remember what it meant. I feel the same about the word 'nature'. Forty-five years ago in the reception class of my rural English primary school we had a Nature Table: a collection of pine cones, catkins in a jar of clouding water, a bird's nest, a bone from a small animal... No doubt a copy of Wordsworth's 'The Daffodils' was pinned to the wall behind it. What the educational purpose of the table would have been I'm not sure: I remember it as a sort of punishment. Unlike the living world outside the classroom, the Nature Table was unreal, uninteresting and dustily dead. Naming it, even now, stirs an old feeling of resentful ennui. Likewise, the phrase 'nature poetry' always has made me turn away sharpish. Of course this is a response to a stereotype of language, not the reality of some poems, but I guess my personal experience is representative of many readers: it may be a category error but it still puts you off. In England when we say 'nature poetry' we think 'Wordsworth', and when we think 'Wordsworth' we mainly mean 'The Daffodils', and generally speaking our hearts don't lift up. So my question is: would you take up an 8,000-line poem by the writer of 'The Daffodils'?

I ask because recently I found myself recommending *The Prelude* to a painter whose work reminds me of Wordsworth. But as the words were leaving my mouth I realised what a hard task *The Prelude* would be for anyone not already part of that very tiny proportion of the population – academics, old-fashioned aficionados and a few poets – who read Wordsworth. Getting into a new author, especially a poet (and even more especially a long poem), requires us to overcome certain anxieties before we are free to start. These anxieties are perversely to do with our everyday security in the medium used by poets. Language that isn't everyday-communicative makes us feel uncomfortable, creating as it does difficulty in an area in which most of us – certainly most readers of this magazine – feel confident: we have vocabulary and syntax at our disposal and humiliating and wasteful it seems to have to undo our confidence. It is hard simply to ignorantly immerse ourselves. The other arts don't have this obstacle. If a musician were to say to me for example, 'Do you know the work of Gerald Finzi? I think you'd like his clarinet concerto', I could buy a CD and try it, somewhat passively, in the privacy of my car for a week. If someone told me I'd enjoy the work of a visual artist, I could go and look in a gallery or get a book or catalogue. I don't have to get past my own relation to paint or colour first. I'm not saying effort – practical, intellectual and creative – isn't required by other art forms, simply that it is easier with them to make a start in a more tangential, less guarded way – you look, listen, watch and maybe develop a taste for them. There are other problems too: beyond the language difficulty, serious literature comes trailing clouds of misapprehension. Some academics have developed a deadly specialised language with which to deal with the raw material of literature, as if removal from what Wordsworth called plainly 'the language of men' gave them a genuinely scientific seriousness. But it's not science we need here. Subject to academic study, as with the Nature Table, literature can look dead and unreal. So where to go for help?

What is needed in a reader is nothing more than a primary confidence (I *can* read this) and a slow mindfulness open to rhythms other than the habitual fast beat of our contemporary busyness. Wendell Berry, the American poet, essayist and thinker, argues for this slowing down as one of the key offerings of a literary discipline. Its 'great practical use', he writes in his essay 'Standing By Words', is

> to slow language down and make it thoughtful… Verse checks the merely impulsive flow of speech, subjects it to another pulse, to measure, to extra-linguistic considerations; by inducing the hesitations of difficulty, it admits into language the influence of the Muse and of musing.

Children naturally have this capacity to work out of focus: moments of abstraction playing with water or sand, blank gazings, lostness… Adults may have it too given the right conditions: set before a huge view, a mass of water, or a winter fire. It's unfortunate that musing is not much valued in our public world (and it is particularly downgraded in the world of education) because the first skill in starting to read a long poem is making yourself go slowly enough. Students of literature are no longer encouraged, if they ever really were, to read in this slowly mindful way. Indeed they are hardly encouraged to read at all: students learn about Wordsworth and how to place him theoretically but they don't learn, unless very lucky, to read him. All of which is to say, you may be much better off as a reader of Wordsworth, or any other writer, if you are reading outside the education system. Down with Nature Tables. Up with a long walk in the hills.

So get an edition of *The Prelude* (there are different versions. I prefer the 1805). Don't read the table of dates, the introduction, or any of the other paraphernalia. Open at Book First, 'Childhood and School Time', and read the first couple of sentences:

> O there is blessing in this gentle breeze
> That blows from the green fields and from the clouds
> And from the sky: it beats against my cheek,
> And seems half-conscious of the joy it gives.
> O welcome messenger! O welcome friend!
> A captive greets thee, coming from a house
> Of bondage, from yon city's walls set free,
> A prison where he hath been long immured.

All you need to start are questions and we only need look for answers in the writing itself. If there aren't any to be found then we go on, in a life-like state of uncertainty, not knowing. In this poem it seems we begin inside a consciousness. When we read 'O there is blessing in this gentle breeze' we are thinking someone's thoughts. It's an amazingly modern informality that plunges us immediately into a mind, even though we don't know who this person is, where he is, or what he's doing. What we are most conscious of is the active and restorative nature of the air – an agent in what Wordsworth will later call 'this active universe'. The breeze carries 'blessing', a word used here with natural ease, as if colloquially, but raising huge questions – what is it to be 'blessed'? who or what performs the 'blessing'? – which Wordsworth leaves unspoken for now. The word is a kind of shorthand, a mark which can be returned to, a marker keeping a thought open. The necessity to accept this shorthand is one of a long poem's most demanding challenges, especially at the beginning where we feel the need to find a footing within the poem. It is hard to keep accepting meanings as provisional.

I like the word 'yon' in line 7, the first mapping word. What can be seen from the eyes we have opened? Green fields, clouds, sky – that's all, but 'yon' places us somewhere in relation to something: we are away from, looking back on, a city. There's a fierce sense of escape from the words 'captive', 'house of bondage', 'set free', 'prison', 'immured'. We know nothing of the terms and nature of the captivity but most readers will recognise the feeling of having been set free, even if only for the weekend. Wonderful to be windswept then.

That's a fleeting start on *The Prelude*, but how about a contemporary fiction? Long-time readers will know of my unhappy search for a great contemporary novel. What is there to match Doris Lessing's hugeness of vision in the *Canopus in Argos* series? *Shikasta* is twenty-five years old. For me there hasn't been a novel of such power since, or rather, there hadn't been until I read *Gilead* by Marilyn Robinson. American readers will know *Gilead* has won the Pulitzer Prize, and many of you will have read the novel. English readers may remember a few ecstatic reviews a couple of months ago. I ignored them on the basis that a modish success would definitely not be to my taste. Wrong. This short, huge, loving, precise and beautiful novel may be the novel Wordsworth would have written if he were alive now and living in Iowa. Its subject is one man's life, journey, and death. It is full of love. My fellow editor, Brian Nellist, tells me my taste has become too metaphysical – the book is 'the most Christian novel I've ever read'. To me Gilead had seemed simply human. True, the protagonist is a preacher – he comes from a veritable tribe of preachers and his life consists of writing sermons and preaching, tending his flock, loving his wife and son, praying to and thinking about God. All the same, I had not thought it a novel about Christianity so much as one about love or devotion or concentration: being here in the world, working out what that is. A man nearly eighty faces death and it fills him with an absolute love of life:

> I really can't tell what's beautiful any more. I passed two young fellows on the street the other day. I know who they are, they work at the garage. They're not churchgoing, either one of them, just decent rascally young fellows who have to be joking all the time, and there they were, propped against the garage wall in the sunshine, lighting up their cigarettes. They're always so black and so strong with gasoline I don't know why they don't catch fire themselves. They were passing remarks back and forth the way they do and laughing that wicked way they have. And it seemed beautiful to me. It is an amazing thing to watch people laugh, the way it sort of takes them over. Sometimes they really do struggle with it. I see that in church often enough. So I wonder what it is and where it comes from, and I wonder what it expends out of your system, so that you have to do it till you're done, like crying in a way, I suppose, except that laughter is much more easily spent.

The novel takes the form of a letter the Reverend John Ames is writing to his son, a child not quite seven years old, so that after his imminent death, there will be something of the father left for the child as he grows up and enters manhood:

> One great benefit of a religious vocation is that it helps you concentrate. It gives you a good basic sense of what is being asked of you and also what you might as well ignore. If I have any wisdom to offer, this is a fair part of it.

John Ames' life as we experience it through this letter is an act of mindfulness: uncertain, courageous, provisional, and in the world. His vocation is essentially active, a means of finding 'what is being asked of you', and though this sounds like a duty the consequence is deeply freeing. His life is the richer for his concentration on small and ordinary things that restores to them their right enormous size. Look back to the epiphanic loveliness of those mechanics: it is as if Ames' eyes were spontaneously, helplessly wealthy, 'I really can't tell what's beautiful any more'. You can hear Wordsworth everywhere in *Gilead*, blessing in the gentle breeze. Is this sense of beauty, of love, in ordinary life part of his vocation as a man of God or simply as a man?

Ames writes, for example, an account of his pastoral relation with his namesake godson John Boughton, a troubled, difficult and disappointing son to Ames' best friend, then comments:

> You might wonder about my pastoral discretion, writing all this out. Well, on one hand, it is the way I have of considering things. On the other hand, he is a man about whom you may never hear one good word, and I just don't know another way to let you see the beauty there is in him.

I find it very moving that the word here is 'beauty' rather than 'goodness', which is what we might expect a pastor to be looking for in a fellow human. Beauty feels involuntary, as if one could never judge, weigh or compare it. Boughton is simply himself, complex and uncategorisable, and that individuation is in itself a large part of the beauty Ames is seeing in all things. I have only read *Gilead* once, and I'm not sure why 'beauty' seems a corollary of 'love'. I only know that 'beauty' is a word given a fuller meaning by this book. John Ames, like one of Wordsworth's gigantic poet/shepherds, is always getting more than the surface from the surface of things:

> in a world of life they live,
> By sensible impressions not enthralled,
> But quickened, rouzed, and made thereby more fit
> To hold communion with the invisible world.

Ames is a man quickened by the experience of life – real mistakes and bad ones too, as well as attempts at generosity and braveness – and the closer he gets to dying the more alive he and the whole world seem. This novel is the finest sort of Nature poetry, concentrated on seeing the dust we are but never dusty.

A Poem by Stephen Newman

London Road

Outside the hospital in Liverpool
I saw a girl – no more than seventeen;
She must have been a few weeks out of school.
Her thin left hand was destitute of ring.
She pushed a buggy, while the blowing wind
And rain lashed down and thrust her coat between
Her legs and moulded her pregnant shape
With such erotic grace that I, heart-thinned
To nothing by a private grief, called out,
'You'll never know how beautiful you are.'
Words are not enough to tell the thing.
She turned her scarf-capped head as if to escape
A blow, and rain and tears poured in a spout
Down her wet-scarred cheeks. And then she hurried far
Off through the storm.
                Poor desolation's daughter,
Waif and naiad whom loss, disaster smother,
Too young and too unskilled to be a mother,
She melted into night: such grace, so much of water.

Gardens of Power and the Power of Gardens

Neil Curry

I have checked since in my dictionary, and I was right. There never was a Latin word for cosy. It just wasn't a concept the Romans rated very highly. *Massive* and *magnificent*, yes; *cosy*, no. This thought crept by me while I was trying to get to grips with another Latin word: *villa*.

Driving east from Rome along the Via Tiburtina towards Tivoli you begin to see the signs for the *Villa Adriana*, but when you get there, you find that Hadrian's villa was not some quiet little place in the country where he could entertain a few friends for the weekend, with fresh figs for breakfast, and so on. Nor was it a palace like the Villa d'Este. No, Hadrian's Villa was a huge, rambling city, and in its heyday, around 138 AD, it was five times bigger than the imperial centre of Rome.

It's all in ruins now, but what ruins: theatres and council chambers, libraries and banqueting halls, as well as the more mundane but necessary things like storerooms, barrack blocks and stables. And everywhere you go there is water: pools and fountains and lakes. One lake alone, in the 'Canopus', is a hundred yards long at least. Magnificent and massive.

And to judge from the statuary, the Romans preferred their women to be on the large size too. *Matronly* certainly comes from a Latin word. But did women have much of a say in the way life was lived in Hadrian's city? The bath-houses and banqueting halls have a very masculine air to them – something of a locker-room syndrome, suggesting all the horseplay of an officers' mess, only writ very large indeed.

But why did he need to build such a place? Politically it might have been an astute move to have the entire imperial court somewhere where they could be kept a close eye on, but it's clear that he also had a passion for architecture. Hadrian didn't only build walls.

It has been claimed that he was the most sensitive and imaginative of the emperors: erudite, with a reputation as a musician, painter, poet and philosopher, yet one who in his early days could, and did, command a legion. A complex man, gloomy and ambitious. Building a 700-acre city for himself may have satisfied one ambition, but you can feel the egocentricity behind it. Hadrian would, I think, have been in complete agreement with what Wallace Stevens wrote in his poem *Theory*:

> I am what is around me.
>
> Women understand this.
> One is not a duchess
> A hundred yards from a carriage.

And if this is true of a duchess, it is even more true of an emperor. You have to be *seen* to be the emperor.

Duchess or no, if women counted for little in Hadrian's 'Villa', they have counted for next to nothing in the Vatican. A country in its own right, the Vatican is smaller than Hadrian's villa-cum-city and there is very little that could be considered ostentatious about its gardens. By tradition, in front of the Governatoro there is the reigning pontiff's coat of arms composed of flowers and boxwood. There is the gentle pseudo-rusticity of an English garden – I suppose you only need to build Arcadia when your reality is Rome – lots of clipped ilex and two or three fountains worth photographing, but you can't help thinking of just how much is missing: obliterated by building.

There was woodland once on the Vatican Hill when Nicholas III, the first Pope ever to do so, took up residence there in 1277. He quickly chopped it down to build himself a walled kitchen garden and to put in an orchard. His successor planted 'simples' and so started the oldest botanical garden in Italy. These men were practical gardeners who knew what they needed, and then Urban V recognised what had so far been missing: he created a vineyard.

But all this has gone. When the Vatican became an independent sovereign state in 1929, government became more important than gardening and we now have a brutal, four-storey administrative headquarters, a railway station, the Vatican Radio Tower, art galleries, museums, and, most recent of all, a heliport.

As you listen to the guide, the gardens begin to sound like a trophy room where the world's gifts and tributes to the Pope have been put on display; from a 'Chinese Pavilion' and a reproduction of the Grotto at Lourdes, to a fragment of the Berlin Wall.

Seemingly, whatever was green and natural could be done without or would have to do what it was told. The most remarkable example of this was the transportation in 1999 of two five-hundred-year-old olive trees from Puglia all the way to St Peter's Square to stand either side of the Pope's altar at Easter. They were then replanted in the garden, and though showing their age, they look likely to survive.

Being elected Pope ensures a place in history; failing to be elected is something that needs to be compensated for, and this, I think, is the story behind the creation of the gardens of the Villa d'Este.

Ippolito d'Este's credentials were awesome. The son of Lucrezia Borgia and grandson of Pope Alexander VI, he was a bishop at the age of 2, an archbishop when he was 10, and a cardinal by the age of 30, but in 1550 the vote went against him and his rival, the new Pope Julius III, appointed him governor of Tivoli. As governors were obliged to remain in the province they governed, he had been virtually exiled, but his response (revenge?) was the garden of the Villa d'Este, the apogee of Italian High Renaissance and so grandiose as to far surpass anything the Pope could boast of in Rome.

Yet is it a garden or a piece of architecture? The dominant effect is not of greenery but of stone: alleys, stairways and balustrades, statues and fountains. Five hundred fountains. In the Villa d'Este water is not permitted simply to flow as it wishes; it is made to spurt, soar, plunge, and cascade. It is a hydraulic masterpiece, a testimony to the power and ingenuity of man. And yet, what makes the fountains so supremely beautiful today is not the shapes they were carved into, but the shapes they have been softened into by the growth of liverwort and moss, lichen and maidenhair. It is as if nature has decided to fight back – as though the Green Man has somehow climbed back in over the wall.

Emperors, popes and cardinals, the gardens I had looked at so far had all been the work of men, and so, heading for the coast, to Tor San Lorenzo, I wondered if the *Giardini della Landriana*, being largely the creation of one woman, would be different. They were, but not in the way I expected.

As recently as 1956, when the Marchesa Lavinia Taverna bought it, it was just twenty-five acres of marshy swamp, which she set about transforming, not into one garden, but into over thirty separate gardens, which the guide, as she conducts you through them, refers to as 'rooms'. And that is a very telling word, as this garden too speaks to us of power, not the power of princes and politicians, but the power of a wealthy woman. These *are* rooms. This is a garden that has been *domesticated.* In the *Giardino degli Aranci*, the two central maples, the eight balanced orange trees and the countless little boxwood shrubs have all been manicured – perfectly and symmetrically rounded.

It is a sensuous and beautiful garden. There are flowers everywhere, but it is as if they are accessories: they match; they have been colour-coordinated. All the roses are pink. There is a blue meadow, a white walk and a grey garden. I have never seen a garden with so many ground-cover plants. The Marchesa did not like to see soil – soil is dirt.

The Landriana as a whole is picturesque, but it is so because it is like a picture gallery. Each separate garden has an individual number and they are meant to be looked at in a specified order, and from a particular place and at a particular angle. The informality could hardly be more formal. It is not a garden that you explore.

One garden I could spend a lifetime exploring is Ninfa. A gift from the Pope to the powerful Caetani family at the close of the thirteenth century, Ninfa became within the next hundred years a flourishing and prosperous city. Inside its fortified walls there were at least seven churches, a castle, a town hall and well over a hundred other civic buildings and houses. But in 1382 the Caetani family were caught up in the Catholic wars of the Great Schism. Ninfa was attacked by the forces of the 'anti-Pope', Clement VII, and totally destroyed. Its inhabitants, those who weren't killed, all fled. The buildings slowly fell further and further into ruin; the wilderness renewed its old authority, and so it stayed for five hundred years and more. But throughout all that time Ninfa remained in the Caetani family, and eventually they came back for it.

It began in the 1920s, and this time it was the work not of one, but of three duchesses – three generations of women who possessed what is perhaps the greatest of all powers: the power of the imagination. Through them a ruined town was transformed into the most romantic of gardens.

To add some romance to their gardens, designers have, in the past, taken to building ruins and bridges, temples and torrents. Ninfa already had them. Once the wilderness was cleared, the family brought back a degree of nurture, but they never lost their faith in nature. Magnolias and roses were introduced and an avenue of cypresses was planted, but clematis was given the freedom of the walls and daisies and even dandelions allowed to flourish where they will.

There is a feeling of something almost sacred about the garden of Ninfa today: people talk quietly there. And I think it is largely due to this sense of balance. The trees and the flowers complement – they do not dominate – the ruins of the ancient city. There is no awareness of a plan, or even of the immense hard work that must have gone into the creation of this garden. It is a kind of controlled disorder. What began as a consequence of war is now at peace with itself.

I have already quoted once from Wallace Stevens, and on another occasion he wrote, 'The trouble with the idea of heaven is that it is merely an idea of the earth.' There are times – and walking through the gardens of Ninfa was one of those times – when I really have no trouble at all with that.

Two Poems by Jacob Polley

Rain

as fishing nets, a wedding dress,
rain that defies rain's downwardness
and spools past the windows, frame by frame –
film after film of Edwardian rain.
Rain as a haunting, rain's ghost-train,
rain bleeding black from the cracks in bricked-up chimneybreasts,
rain's wall-maps, rain's damp lands outlined in great stains.

Old rain, the same rain, my father's father's cold rain
taken up like a tune, confessed
to the city, committed to the drains
and the dark and piped as one body under playgrounds and
cold-frames.
From the hills comes rain as more river, not falling
but fattening; bales of newspapers, abandoned books,
hemp ropes and halters of fungi. Rain feeds.

From the top bar of a five bar gate hangs
a moment's perfectly-achieved water seed
while the river slides by, echoing and echoey.
Rain as lost shoes, drinkers huddled like rooks;
rain that's put paid, done you out of a day; rain's patter, rain's slang,
rain's be-spittling of a spider's web.
Rain's pillars of smoke, rain's rooms outside the room

you watch from as rain runs through its embodiments –
a bride swinging like a bell, a lunch-hour factory crowd,
the shadow of a matchstick girl: the smudgy, underdeveloped dead
rain remembers as spaces it once rained around.

Rain's pencil leads, rain's sketchiness,
rain writing but whatever it tries to read back
drowned out. Rain's inconsequence to the sea.

A few pins drop then rain's loosened like hair
or it steps clean out of the air.
Rain's sound is the sound of the world unwrapped
and unwrapped from reams of cellophane.
But in the near-silence of just-halted rain,
the black earth of any common field lies –
frankincense for whoever passes by.

Grass

grows on roofs, from gutters.
  The verges hunger
and nod *yes, yes, the wind is green,*
  the light's for eating:
we wear men out with our growing.

Lasting Interest in Everything

Les Murray talks to Jane Davis about how he learned to read

Do you remember learning to read?
I must have been about three years old and I began to notice that there were letters. They appeared in streams under things and on packages and so on, and I think the first words I can remember reading were 'g-o-l-d-e-n s-y-r-u-p' which was commonly sold by the CSR company in Australia, sugar manufacturers, and people used golden syrup a lot in cooking, and I started doing this, working out various phrases and getting the sound of them. So my mother got me a little cloth book of the alphabet and I puzzled that out and started slowly reading bits of the newspapers – particularly the comics.

Do you remember looking at that book with your mother?
No, I remember looking at it by myself; it was a cloth book, very sturdy. I can remember reading the war news in the papers, after a while I was reading the captions under the photographs, you see, of the war which was going on at the time. But particularly I loved the comic strips, of which there were many in the papers then. And then I moved to my mother's set of encyclopaedias – Cassell's Children's Encyclopaedia for 1924 which she'd won at school and it was in 8 volumes and I can still remember the abbreviations on the spines of the books telling you the area of the alphabet each one covered. They went [he tells me like a man reciting a poem, very rhythmically] a to boa, boa to con, coo to flo, flo to isis, ita to nav, nav to sca, sca to zwi and Index. I read everything in those books, I read them until they fell apart, and got a lasting interest in everything. And only poetry will fit an encyclopaedic mind.

Was there any poetry in the encyclopaedia?
Only retellings of some of Homer's stories. They got picked up – my father actually was fascinated by the story of the Cyclops. He was a great natural storyteller and used to make up his own stories. But

that one appealed to him – one master storyteller to another...he incorporated that one in his repertoire. He was not a man of the written culture at all; he actually forgot how to read. He left school at fourteen, got married at twenty-eight and picked up the newspaper on his honeymoon and found to his chagrin that he could not read it. He said it took him two or three days to get the trick back. He never read much, reckoned he only read half a book in his life. I'm prepared to believe it.

What about the Bible, was that around?
He didn't read that, no. He heard it. He swore by it, quite literally. When he was in a fury biblical phrases would come tearing out of him: 'I can't bloody deal with him. Man that is born of bloody woman, couldn't deal with him!' 'All the days of his bloody life...' It gave a kind of mad dignity to the swearing. They were all like that – they were soaked in the Bible, Wee free, Free Kirk Presbyterians.

Was your mother Free Kirk?
No, Anglican. One of her strongest religious principles was dislike of Catholics. Mainly because she'd had a great row with the Mother Superior of a school she was sent to and it would have been the meeting of two dreadnoughts at full steam because they were both very tough, very determined women one of them only sixteen and the other one grown up but they must have had a terrible knock-down, drag-out... And so she was always pretty prejudiced against Catholics. My father loyally supported that – he'd been brought up on anti-Catholicism himself.

What was it like then when you became a Catholic?
Must have been terrible because he never mentioned it. In forty, in more than forty years, he never raised the subject, or never raised it with me anyway. One time I was talking to my German translator, Margitt, and I said 'You know in all those years he never mentioned my conversion,' and she said, 'He mightn't have mentioned it to you but he mentioned it to me.' 'Oh,' I said, 'By gum, did he?' 'Yeah,' she said. 'You and Valerie had gone off to Mass and he turned to me and he said "I don't bloody know why he turned Catholic."' So I said to Margitt, 'Well, he could have asked me.' And somehow I had a constraint about it too, I wasn't going to raise it unless he raised it, and he wasn't going to raise it unless I raised it. We did have one or two very generalised religious conversations very late in his life in his last four months. They weren't very long. One of them was 'Dad, have you forgiven your enemies? Your father and all them?' People who used to haunt his mind with kind of obsessive force,

a long quarrel that had gone on. He said 'Oh, I must have, I don't think about that now.' And I said, 'You old fraud, you mean you can forgive people without noticing?' He said, 'Looks like it, don't it?' That was that conversation. I can't remember the others… that was the main one.

Go on about the encyclopaedia, go back…
It was black and white. I can't remember that there were many tipped-in colour pages, I think there were a few, a very few. Mock photography, drawings made to look like photographs…

I had one of those – Arthur Mee's Children's Encyclopaedia…
I had that one later – that was about 8 volumes too.

I've still got mine. I can remember reading things and thinking I don't understand this… There must be things you don't understand.
You read it again. I suppose it is part of the package. You don't understand it that time but next time round you read it again. You read other things. I was always quite undiscriminating in reading. I'd read comic books and Charles Darwin at the same time. Charles Darwin happened to come into my hands when I was about nine. I found it great; I enjoyed it. Occasionally books of that weight would come along and then you'd be reading other stuff in between.

People would give them to you?
You'd find them. There was a schoolteacher called Pascoe down the road staying at my aunt Edna's place, my favourite auntie's place, and I plagued Mr Pascoe for the lend of about half his books until then finally he got mean and wouldn't lend them anymore; I think he was a bit jealous that I was reading them and he wasn't. He just had them as a possession and I was actually sucking out the content.

Were you going to school at that point?
By the time I met Pascoe I was. I went to school at the age of nine. There were no schools around within reach. It didn't matter because I was a self-educator. I read everything that come along. Except maths. I had a blind spot for it and when I got to school it was not a curable blind spot. They managed to hammer a bit into me. The schoolteacher himself was only a boy about nineteen, straight from teachers' college, and there were sixteen of us at the school and I turned up on the first day with an essay on the Vikings. Thinking that's what you do at school, you write essays… So he didn't know what the hell to do with this and he read it out to the class and they didn't know what to do with it. So the whole matter was passed over

in silence. I didn't do that again. I didn't really mean to show off – I just thought that's what you did. I didn't see many other people at that time, child or any others. I saw my Catholic girl cousins I was fond of and my cousin Tasman Arnall once or twice a year. I can't remember very many other people.

So being in a class of sixteen kids…
We didn't have classes – littlies being taught to read and the rest of us being given stuff to keep us occupied. There wasn't enough to do. I've always found that's true of school, the slow learners drag everyone down and there's not enough to do. So you start playing truant. I truanted my way through the next couple of years… at Nabiac Central School. Nabiac was nice because we were young teenagers. We were fairly innocent. We went to school barefoot, no school uniform, 150 kids all up from kindergarten to intermediate certificate, which was half way through the high school, and it was known that I would come to school on Wednesdays because that was the day they had educational films – this was before television; there was no television in Australia then. And any other day I was likely to be absent, at home or under the bridge reading, or off shooting rabbits. That's what you did in the fifties, you shot rabbits – rabbits were taking over Australia and you shot them… but we were fooling ourselves, we couldn't shoot enough rabbits. What finally shot them was a disease called myxomatosis.

Do you remember when you first read poetry?
I read it sporadically, I suppose, all through. Occasionally would be vaguely interested, thinking this is a funny way of telling a story but it sounds a bit like the Bible, heightened language. I hadn't figured out my reactions to it entirely

So it was stories you'd read – it was narrative?
It would tend to be narrative poetry, yes. I remember reading 'The Ancient Mariner' in some connection that way and I very much liked it. I read Milton in a weekend, the whole of him. Three-day weekend. Sucked it all down.

How old would you be then?
Fifteen. Never read him again. Immunised myself! I wasn't entirely sure it wasn't a continuation of the Bible. But we weren't much interested in the poetry served up in school because – good stuff though it was – it related to England two hundred years ago. What they call country house poetry. It had no relation to our life at all. It was just part of the course of civilising us that they thought they had to do.

When I struck modern poetry, I think it was a fairly pastoral event, it took me several years to realise it. I was known by some of the teachers to be having a hell of a time at the hands of some of my fellow students, and having no resources much to combat it. And instead of intervening, which doesn't work, one or two of them did me favours and the great favour that a fellow called McLoughlin did was to introduce me to modern poetry. I think that was my compensation for being routinely crucified by the girls. Then the sports master mentioned that there was not only modern poetry – there was modern Australian poetry. Les Laurie his name was. I thought Australian poetry consisted entirely of bush ballads, if I thought about it at all. Then I was introduced to regular modern poetry by Australians that was about things that I knew and familiar scenes and all that. I remember the first poem was one by a fellow named Doug Stewart who actually was a New Zealander in exile, writing about Aboriginal carvings around Sydney. They are very ancient figurative carvings on the flat rock surfaces around Sydney, and fascinating they are, echidnas, fish, the sun, a man inside a whale, all sorts of things, I was fascinated by that. I'd have been about eighteen when that revelation occurred. And I thought 'I can do this.' And I've been trying to prove it ever since.

But newspapers were part of the reading too and Mum got various magazines, she got the old *Women's Weekly* which still exists but it comes out monthly… and she got *The Australian Journal* which was a short story magazine. The stories were good. And we used to see the old *The Bulletin* which was a curious kind of magazine: it was full of topical items from the countryside and it had what was the red page – the out covers of it were pink and literary content on the pink pages…

Did you have a radio at home?

We did. It stood up about three and half feet high, was a big cabinet radio, great big old valves inside it and the aerial was a piece of fencing wire strung between high poles and we'd pull in the whole world, put it on short wave. Could hear China, Germany, coming in whispering and burbling at night. We listened to radio; you'd sit around the radio exactly the way people sit around television.

Bush ballads – did you hear people sing them, or say them?

They recited them at dances, parties, privately round the table. A lot of country people still do. There is probably more of a market in Australia for bush balladry than there is for snob verse and a lot of poets have dipped in there to learn bits and pieces. One thing the bush ballads never do is dip into us to learn us. They're still being produced but the problem is they are still stuck in 1880, with occasional modern technology in it. Instead of overcoming a problem with a team of bullocks you might be overcoming problems with a Mac diesel truck. But the spirit is exactly the same. Quite popular still.

What did your Mum and Dad think of your self-educating?
They were enormously proud of this weird clever child they had and said that I should be further educated. I don't know how real that was to Dad – he lived entirely in his world of ballroom dancing and storytelling and gossip and he recited bush ballads – Banjo Patterson and the like. But Mum she came from the city and a slightly different world, a world of print and technological vocabulary. From my mother I got print and any sense I might have. The old man never had much sense. She approved of my reading. She didn't entirely approve of me in some ways but she approved of my head… I think that she was embittered gradually by her series of miscarriages and the whole business of children and childbearing became a bit of a horror to her. I think the suspicion was that my birth had made Mum's womb incompetent. I was induced because of a woman called Cheers. Mrs Wilga Cheers – Wilga is a species of flowering Australian plant. I never met the lady, but she had what they call a weak heart. Wilga Cheers died the other day in her eighties so it couldn't have been too bad a heart, but she was pregnant and there was this little cottage hospital for mothers and babies, a lying-in hospital and Mum went in and Wilga Cheers was there and they said 'We may need all our resources – we haven't got many – for Mrs Cheers when she starts to give birth because her heart may give trouble at the same time. So your baby is over term anyway, what do you think about our inducing it?' Of course Mum was an ex-nurse, a good one and she was the sort of person who was likely to be swayed by medical terminology. So Dr Stokes induced me one morning in October 1938 and ever after that she had only miscarriages. There may have been no connection. Wilga Cheers had her baby two days later with not the slightest problem. I hope she had a lot of babies. That's about all I can remember about learning to read. It didn't ever seem hard. It seemed worthwhile.

What you've described seems a strange mixture of facts, the encyclopaedia and narratives. That's reflected in your poetry, isn't it?
I was always fond of facts because facts give you power. They give you a sense of being on top of things.

Four Poems by Jane Routh

A woman visits the young letter-writer in Shaanxi Province

I keep my promise, this is what I want to tell him.
No please, change that, write: all my promises.
Tell him the peaches will be small this year
and not so many; next week I shall take some
to the village. He used to carry them for me,
everyone knew. You will have seen him yourself.
Now I only manage two baskets for the market.
No, this is not to be written: I do not complain.

Write that the Bedford Van stands still in the yard;
I keep a little diesel, but no one has his trick
to start her. You have not learned the word for trick?
No matter, tell him she is now a cupboard!
His pickaxe, spade, bucket of nails, all are inside
and dry, even when the floodwaters came.
Your mother says my own things should be
kept in there, but that is not my way.

You were here that day, too? How fast the waters
overtook the streets – tell him about chasing watermelons,
the red-brown colour of the water, and people running.
I was not frightened by the flood, only by the sky,
the way night fell in the afternoon,
so dark, and the only sound was rain.
Do you remember that queer light later
in the west, that felt like being watched?

I wonder if there are floods in his country;
perhaps this is why I have no news.
No. No, all this is talk. After the Bedford Van, write

that he would not know her: tell him she is tidy
and I paint her blue, all over blue of the sky at dusk
we used to see from the bed. Now I cannot see the sky,
only the Bedford Van close by the window,
but the same blue as the sky when he was here.

The Reedbed

What was I hoping for, what was I trying to find
that September afternoon, skimming across
the Humber under slender cables to the other side.
That past of course, something to say this is how it was,
even something forgotten of my own, a view perhaps,
to account for how I imagine ships trawl
the top of an embankment beyond a kitchen window.
But there were no ships. All that brown water
and just a green-hulled light-float with its silent bell.

What was there to see in a village of closed doors
gone about its twenty-first century commute.
The church was locked. Not one headstone shared my name.
Behold, he taketh away; who can say unto him, what dost thou.
A gable end stopped me – not familiar, but seen before.
I'd gone because I still love the colour of bottled plums,
the press of golden flesh through crimson juice against glass.
I did find the orchards, now The Orchards, meaning
executive houses instead of trees. And one old brick wall.

On the sign outside The Ferryboat, one man rows another
across the estuary, all that distance in a little yellow hull.
But where the boatyard was, ploughed stubble.
No voices, no hammering, no trace of planking or a nail;
nothing to write home about as my father would have said.
Only the reeds, their grey plumes and dry leaves
lilting in the sun with a sound like running water
tell how it was then. The tall, plumed reeds.

Night and Day

Strange, to wake back in middle age, stiff and sore.
If we inhabited our lives the other way round
with the colour and contrast turned up full,
Pharaoh's armourer offering to cut off our rings
with bolt cutters, against a backdrop of gold pyramids,
no they're palm trees, I mean doors,
everyone we know using everyone else's name
and acting out of character with intimate strangers
kicking up divots from long ago, the ground tilting
the car hurtling backwards down the track
even though it's in first gear, no brakes at all,
we'd be exhausted and long for our dream days:
the kettle in the right place, breakfast always the same,
our weekly shop, even the slow pulse of the seasons
lending a little glow of predictability;
we'd love the washing-up bowl, the settee,
grey days, no wind, and especially fog.
A small price, the body, we'd say, taking our pills.

Wind in the Willows

He demands the whole of the first chapter
every night. We tire, and buy him the tape.
Every night he rewinds and replays the picnic.
He's never had cold tongue or pickled gherkins:
it must have been the way she used to show him
the words on the page and take such a deep breath.
He'd gulp and recite along but couldn't get past
cresssandwiches. His brother's too young
to be much use, though is addressed as *Mole.*
Now he commands her garden bench, sculls it
upriver with her hoe and a broom,
walks on water to moor it to the apple tree
then runs for wellies to keep his feet dry.
He wades back stiff-legged in her old ones,
climbs aboard and lies still a long while.
Ahoy there! I ask if he's OK. *Get off, get off.*
There's no softness in him. She always said
school would change him. How I miss her.

Hardy and Landscape

Ralph Pite

Osip Mandelstam, the Russian poet, wrote this in 1923 about how people see landscapes:

> We look at the forest and we say
> here are many ships already in the trees, masts,
> the red pines
> bare of their rough burden clear to the top,
> they should creak in the storm
> like solitary pines,
> in the raging treeless air.
> ('He who finds a horseshoe')

When we look at woodland – the woods seen from the bus or the train, or the forests in nature programmes – Mandelstam says we see something else: not the woods themselves but what we can make out of them, ships and masts instead of trunks. Keats implied the same habit of exploitativeness when he described Isabella's wicked brothers as 'the hawks of ship-mast forests'. Similarly, Hardy's *The Woodlanders* portrays a forest that is worked, and his characters inhabit nature without losing the point of view that Mandelstam describes. When Giles Winterbourne looks at a forest he sees in the trees spars, hurdles and planks.

Mandelstam takes this idea further by suggesting unacknowledged contradictions and self-deceptions in our ways of seeing. We may look for masts in the trees and yet at the same time we want the trees to stay as they are: 'the red pines [...] should creak [...] like solitary pines'. The simile seems to go back on itself, anti-climactically. It is as if the imagined loss of the trees (converted into masts) allowed their creaking to be imagined more intensely, set in a scene of solitary bleakness.

This is a striking turn in the poem. That people see in nature what they can do with it is not such a strange idea really; it can even be an invigorating one. Mandelstam is concerned with something more uncomfortable though – the idea that we habitually aggrandise the natural world, looking in it and demanding from it images of sublimity. This is a way we have of telling ourselves that our destructive involvement is a kind of ennobling – that we are not altering the trees, we are 'making something' of them (and they ought to be grateful).

Something similar could be said about the way we regard mountains. Historically, mountainous landscapes are the ones people have especially tried to conserve; until recently, all the national parks in England and Wales were in mountain areas and the majority of them still are. When you think of the Yorkshire Dales, the Brecon Beacons and most of all the Lake District, the image that comes to mind is of bare slopes, forbidding and inspiring, that tower above cultivated land and reach into the clouds. The hills are elemental and challenging. Walking among them creates a narrative of struggle and self-exposure, with the chance of final reward – you walk to gain a vision from the heights and/or a confrontation with your true self, in its strengths and weaknesses. You are going, in other words, on a quest.

If, though, the sheep were taken from these mountains, their bare slopes would in time be reforested. The bareness of the hills, which makes them sublime, is man-made, and especially in the Scottish Highlands, it is a very recent change. Eighteenth-century tea-clippers were built on the Moray coast using local wood, which was floated downstream on rivers rising in the Cairngorms. When the forests were exhausted, the shipyards closed. The deforestation helped open up the mountains to visitors and made the Highlands good deer-stalking country but it emptied them of their native fauna and flora, including the native humans, the crofters, who were forced to emigrate. These clearances famously 'created a wilderness and called it peace'; making a wilderness was, paradoxically, a kind of taming.

Some environmentalists are now suggesting that the numbers of sheep and deer should be reduced in upland areas so that the forests can grow back. Changes in the Common Agricultural Policy make this more economically attractive and, of course, growing trees absorb carbon dioxide, contributing to the struggle against global warming. Whether or not that is the best way forward ecologically, it certainly seems as if people looking at Mandelstam's forests or at British mountains seek to make the landscape into a mirror of themselves. They see in it a material resource, whether of wood or grazing land, and a psychological, affective one as well. As the wilderness is conquered in order to put it to use, it yields images of conquest. Trees become symbols of gritty resistance to the elements;

mountains allow us to tell ourselves a story of overcoming the odds to gain final victory. We want, in other words, to commune with this kind of landscape because it shows us what we would like to be. We mould the landscape (both in reality and through our portrayals of it) in such a way that it corresponds to our desires.

Mandelstam's sense of how we look at landscapes is odd (and rather disturbing, I think) because we are more accustomed to assume they stand as a rebuke to our self-importance. Nature is often valued for showing us how small we are. The teenagers sent into the wilds of Utah on *Brat Camp*, for instance, are expected to learn team-spirit, endurance and mutual respect. As this process takes place, the environment is there to help them realise that, spoilt as they may have been, they do not occupy the centre of the world.

One of Hardy's friends as an aspiring writer was Leslie Stephen, editor of the *Cornhill Magazine*, which published *Far From the Madding Crowd* in 1874 and so made Hardy's name. Stephen was already a well-known literary man when Hardy first came across him. He was also a famous walker, who would habitually hike from Cambridge into London and who conquered hitherto unclimbed peaks in the Alps. For Stephen, reaching the summit was a 'feat of manly might' ('Zermatt: To the Matterhorn') in which you 'ventured life and limb' – risking all in the hope of success. '[F]eat of manly might' and 'ventured life and limb' are Hardy's phrases, from poems he wrote about Stephen and the Matterhorn. He perfectly understood Stephen's ambitions as a mountaineer and Stephen's belief that mountaineering was morally useful but he shared some of Mandelstam's hesitation too. The Schreckhorn looks to Hardy less like a 'looming Alp-height' than:

> a guise of him
> Who scaled its horn with ventured life and limb,
> Drawn on by vague imaginings, maybe,
> Of semblance to his personality
> In its quaint glooms, keen lights, and rugged trim.
> ('The Schreckhorn')

Stephen was, as Hardy says of the mountain, a 'spare and desolate figure', especially in later life, when he was widowed, melancholy and unable to save himself from overwork. Hardy suggests too that 'maybe' Stephen sensed the similarity between himself and the mountain and that his feeling of kinship was what drew him on. If so, he was climbing in search of himself; he wanted to accomplish his heroic feats in order to prove that he could live up to his expectations of himself. Nature was his self-image and his double.

Hardy considered this attitude towards landscape again in a later poem, 'After a Romantic Day.' Although for Hardy we live (to borrow his phrase from him) after a romantic day, when the landscape has been stripped of its characteristically Romantic features, its beauty, wildness and 'naturalness', people carry on nevertheless acting Romantically within it:

> The railway bore him through
> An earthen cutting out from a city:
> There was no scope for view,
> Though the frail light shed by a slim young moon
> Fell like a friendly tune.
>
> Fell like a liquid ditty,
> And the blank lack of any charm
> Of landscape did no harm.
> The bald steep cutting, rigid, rough,
> And moon-lit, was enough
> For poetry of place: its weathered face
> Formed a convenient sheet whereon
> The visions of his mind were drawn.

This prosaic, industrialised landscape serves for 'poetry of place' as well as Alpine sublimity does. Where Leslie Stephen found in the mountain something resembling himself, the man leaving the city discovers 'a convenient sheet whereon / The visions of his mind were drawn.' A denuded cutting attracts him precisely because it offers no resistance. An empty landscape – 'earthen', 'blank', 'bald' and 'weathered' – suits us better apparently than one filled up with (and hidden behind) its native vegetation. We like nature cleared because then we can trace on and in it our own preoccupations.

The man in the railway carriage seems more decisive than Stephen had been and more wrapped up in private visions. Landscape is a blank page for him, a canvas for reverie. Vague imaginings of semblance have turned into the mind's visions, drawn on the *tabula rasa* that we have made of the outside world.

The Victorian mountaineer and the 1920s' commuter are, however, more similar than you would expect. Both thrive on barrenness, 'The bald steep cutting' offering one the same opportunity for self-attention as the 'spare and desolate' Schreckhorn does for the other. The difference between the two poems is illustrated by their sharing the word 'drawn'. The Schreckhorn poem employs an ambiguous syntax to give 'drawn on' a double meaning: Stephen is 'drawn on' to climb further 'by vague imaginings' – by the tentative belief that the mountain is a kind of soul-mate; the mountain too, though, can be the subject here for a moment at least. It is 'a guise of' Stephen 'Drawn on by vague imaginings' – inscribed, that is to say, with the meanings Stephen wants to find there.

By bringing together urban and natural like this, prosaic and sublime (something which the second poem does so strikingly through its clashes of register), Hardy suggests that this Romantic address to landscape is surprisingly indifferent to place. The 'blank lack of any charm' in the new world created by industry actually does 'no harm'. If anything it is more 'convenient' for us. The poem suggests that all languages of natural description have become hackneyed: 'the frail light of a slim young moon' invokes a lyricism undercut by the interchangeability of 'friendly tune' (with its Tin-Pan Alley rhyme) and 'liquid ditty'. Only for a moment with 'And moon-lit' does the transformation of the landscape seem external to the self, magical and uncontrived. Yet, amidst its sense of disappointment, there is more fatalism than complaint. The decay of Victorian heroism shifts only the context of self-projection. There's no removing people's self-concern.

Hardy's landscapes characteristically are marked by human footprints. In his first published novel, *Desperate Remedies*, there's a remarkable passage where characters walking along a road at night during heavy rain can tell simply by hearing the different sounds made by the falling raindrops what crops are being grown:

> Sometimes a soaking hiss proclaimed that they were passing by a pasture, then a patter would show that the rain fell upon some large-leafed root crop, then a paddling plash announced the naked arable.

Likewise for someone so interested in landscape, he has surprisingly little to say about wilderness. Nearly all of his landscapes are agricultural; even Egdon Heath, which has escaped the plough, is grazed by ponies and its furze is constantly cut. Hardy's Heath differs essentially from the moors of *Wuthering Heights* because it offers no escape from other people and their prying eyes. His Nature is not opposed to Civilisation because his different landscapes express subtly different traditions of human behaviour. He moves always between kinds of farming – dairy, sheep, forestry, or winter-work in the exposed fields of Flintcomb-Ash. Even his harshest landscapes are populated and man-made, and Hardy does not follow the pattern of Romantic views of nature. He is thoroughly unconvinced that nature at its most elemental brings out the essence of the self. Exposure brings flatness instead. When you pit yourself against nature, as Leslie Stephen had done with his feats of manly might, it turns out you are nothing – not just comparatively but utterly valueless. Henry Knight hanging over the cliff-edge in *A Pair of Blue Eyes* comprehends this, if only momentarily, in the context of geological time. When faced by the immediate prospect of death, he identifies minute fossils in the cliff rocks and thinks: 'He was to be with the small in his death'.

Hardy is a more affirmative writer than is often recognised and he does offer an alternative to this alternation between *hubris* and disappointment. It consists in learning how to enjoy being with the small in your life. Clym Yeobright, when he comes home from Paris in *The Return of the Native*, re-enters his old haunts most fully when, blinded by too much reading, he becomes a furze-cutter, abandoning his idea of founding a school and taking up instead the most humble form of manual labour available. He is so well-disguised by his work-clothes that he can barely be distinguished from the landscape; even his mother recognises him with difficulty. Furthermore, Clym continues to project 'the visions of his mind' onto a landscape even when he seems most absorbed into it.

When working on the heath, Clym's

> Daily life was of a curious microscopic sort, his whole world being limited to a circuit of a few feet from his person. His familiars were creeping and winged things, and they seemed to enrol him in their band. Bees hummed around his ears with an intimate air, and tugged at the heath and furze-flowers at his side in such numbers as to weigh them down to the sod. [...] Tribes of emerald-green grasshoppers leaped over his feet, falling awkwardly on their backs, heads, or hips, like unskilful acrobats, as chance might rule; or engaged themselves in noisy flirtations under the fern-fronds with silent ones of homely hue. Huge flies, ignorant of larders and wire-netting, and quite in a savage state, buzzed about him without knowing that he was a man. [...] Litters of young rabbits came out from their forms to sun themselves upon hillocks, the hot beams blazing through the delicate tissue of each thin-fleshed ear, and firing it to a blood-red transparency in which the veins could be seen.

What is striking about this passage is its mixture of precision and playfulness. Immersed in the primal, pre-historical environment of the heath (whose vegetation, bracken, has remained unchanged since it formed coal), Clym seems to see 'unskilful acrobats' and hear 'noisy flirtations'. Hardy's writing anthropomorphises recklessly and sounds at points archly amused, as for instance when it observes that the flies are 'quite in a savage state'. That phrase is nearly camp. Then, at the close of the paragraph, the description highlights the pathos too of the young rabbits; they are so delicate that the sunlight shines through their ears, revealing a bloody, Darwinian red.

Human interests are always modifying nature in this paragraph; the mind, even when curious and even when looking microscopically, sees imaginatively and subjectively as well. No grasshopper is an acrobat, really, skilful or otherwise, and there is, in nature, no reason to bemoan predation. We project onto nature both the comedy and the tragedy. And oddly, Hardy sounds very positive about this. At his most absorbed, Clym seems also at his freest. Hitherto, he has come across as a rather earnest and Romantic figure. When he casts aside his high-minded ambitions, however, giving up progress and Victorian masculinity at the same moment, he does not lose himself in nature. Instead, dependence on the environment releases a flood of varied, spontaneous, inconsistent responses; it makes possible his creative (and comic) engagement with the life that surrounds him.

Though it is by Victorian standards immoral of Tess to look forward to a happier future once she is a fallen woman, she does so all the same. 'It was unexpended youth, surging up anew after its temporary check, and bringing with it hope, and the invincible instinct towards self-delight.' Clym's daily life as a furze-cutter has just this quality too; as soon as it finds itself no longer checked by a desire to control and improve the natural world, his mind surges up.

In a sense, as in 'After a Romantic Day', the bracken forms another 'convenient sheet whereon / The visions of [a human] mind are drawn' and, especially now, when the human invasion of natural environments seems so appallingly destructive, you can wish intensely that people could learn somehow to stop imposing themselves on the world around. For Hardy, that desire is another symptom of the problem rather than its solution. What his writing in *The Return of the Native* suggests, instead, is a relation to landscape that allows people to become actively a part of the natural world – the human part.

Two Poems by John Kinsella

Swoop (suddenness)

Suddenness a parabola, cut of pendulum,
regionalism we'd imagine;
                                        a steady line
from road to treeline, deletions
of light breeze, dictions of cloud,
irritations coloured out – idols
of *vicious demonstrations...* sweetly
landed; give me a break.
            You take a portion, a magpie's
ripping hardware, parental fire, and curse
the regular: a strengthened dream, prolific
tempering of tabernacle...
                        And then it's done.
Leant against skin
of shed, the metal bar toppled, crashed
against raintank, resounded singularly
across the paddock...
                              pink and greys
dismounted dead limb, shape-wise still a York gum,
and resettled – to the naked eye, flashing
in knee-jerk reaction, precisely back
to where they started.

            An alteration,
then continuance, though swooping magpie,
its nesting ire sanctioned, rips again,
intensified, if anything.
            How do you say: prick of a thing,
I admire you...?
Why bother cosying up to the neighbour

swooping in on his 'special materials' wings,
self-deluded 'angel of evening'.
                    It upsets highly-strung
members of household – a blue enfolding,
white flagged against barbed wire,
                                        raider
moves of magnitude. That's worship
in granary logic – implanting
pleasure, shredding Miltonic absolutes
settled here as warning
    against a love
        of nature. Apprehend
sundew and scarlet runner, outré
on firebreaks...
            apprehend
this swoop against incursion,
raid of logic: as over *strongholds and defences*,
we parry, shout suddener
than we rebuild our pictures,
decorate the senses.

Astonishment

A tract of bush without twists and loops
of dumped product, dead sheep, mounds
of beer bottles, settlement weeds clinging
to a hillside, a single cell of bush concentrating
attention; the rumble of a V8 on bitumen
not far from where you explore a sandy
track, your car parked a short way
into clumps of hakea, where a V8 slowing down
is warning – taking an interest in banksias –
unlikely... the driver glimpsing, processing
brakes and deceleration, those crimes
opportunity and the grotesque feed on,
circumstantial paths almost joined.
Closer to home, bring unreachable wandoos

on the steepest side of Walwalinj closer…
lenses welded through glasses, through eyes…
more intense than being there, taste of terror
enlarged unfamiliar but still perspective
a subject held in the palm of a trickster,
lens his medium, not mechanism,
branching vein structure, brain tissue,
flume of lymph, vertical fan coral
prised out of sediments, the familiar
you barely notice though birds fly up in flocks
and disappear, all colours absorbed – pink and grey,
green-blue-yellow-orange plash of twenty-eights,
minute red-capped robins carrying red
further than background edicts.

In this perverse travelling lived-in countries
form overlapping triptychs despite oceans…
topographies of differing personality traits,
a single image welded and transmogrified,
pungent bacilli you can barely rest up in,
that troubles with comfort of sparrow
or ant trails, blue-tongue lizard lodged
tight in winter sleep: it reminds you,
the smallest difference on re-encounter
astonishes, fills you with that terror,
a salivation of ensconcement,
heteromorph's vision of exile,
roots tapped deeper than rock,
teasing flick or rustled hairline.

By Any Other Name...

John Kinsella

I have a tendency to scare-quotes, out of a need to signal that I am using a word or phrase reflectively, aware of the problems associated with its usage, ironically, or self-consciously. Drop the scare-quotes, and a piece of writing that challenges a particular concept might seem to turn out to support that concept – or so my paranoia tells me. Grammatically, scare-quotes are as much part of the formula as periods or semi-colons, but perhaps their actions are somewhat more fluid. Conventions change rapidly – language evolves – so quotation marks around parts of speech give way to dashes (or no indicative punctuation at all), and commas are generally neglected. To highlight consciousness of a particular word usage, sometimes italics or bolding work as effectively – though, I'd argue, with different emphasis. Then too, the scripts of email have brought the lushness of emoticons to further guide or direct the environment of reception – in case we misunderstand, in that cold and quick medium of email.

I note the scare-quote issue because at the beginning of my volume of poetry *The New Arcadia*, I chose not to scare-quote two tree names: salmon gum and spotted gum. The poem is a 'drive' (there we go) – the first in a series of five poems that track my partner (or someone) driving home to York in the Avon Valley from Western Australia's capital city, Perth. The poem marks a departure from a major road – the Great Eastern Highway – to a less-travelled one – the Great Southern Highway. The point of departure is at a roadhouse called The Lakes (named literally after adjacent lakes) – a V in the road/s. In the poem there is an ambivalence about where the speaker is positioned and where in fact s/he is referring to, but we get the general impression it is about the main road between The Lakes and York (clarified further along in the poem). Then the lines go:

> from cryptic entanglements
> of salmon gums – brief
> but intense stands bristling
> on high ground, to ghostly trunks
> of spotted gum, where firebreaks

then paddocks striate between gravel
and sand...

When composing it, I probably should have scare-quoted the tree types, though I am glad I resisted. Why did I resist? Though not endemic to that stretch of road, salmon gums are not unusual just north of York – 'up this way' – and though technically an eastern states of Australia species, spotted gums are planted on fence-lines and driveways around the district. Furthermore, 'spotted gum' is a childhood and occasional local name for wandoo (or white gum), which grows around York and on the road from The Lakes to York. It is with the nickname that the scare-quotes might come into play. It is a tangled web of location and identity, and the slippage between name and science is one that especially interests me. Why do we name things as we do?

In 2000 I wrote a poem entitled 'Name-loss' in response to an insight of George Seddon's:

Name-loss

The interesting questions about plants are not what they are called nor where they are found, but how they make a living, why they are so different from each other, how they come to look as they do, and why they are found in one place rather than another.

George Seddon, *Sense of Place*

The basic varieties
Stick with you out of childhood,
Or those you've written about:
A reason for persisting.
Within themselves it's immaterial,
The fetish, the vital ingredient
For remedy or potion;
Our need they don't share,
Despite our giving up
Stale breath that they might flourish
And reward us with fresh air.
Name-loss, you tell yourself,
Means nothing: it's how
They live that matters.
And generation on generation
Brings change that makes the name
No longer the same,
If only they'd recognise it.
Like a popular song or item of clothing
Gone out of fashion?

Or special properties
That might heal or comfort
Lungs, stomach, heart,
Left behind in the rush
For synthetics. Out there – diminished –
The hakea, dryandra, grevillea,
Names stripped of their growth,
A place in language.

While deeply admiring Seddon's granting of a certain kind of agency to plants, what particularly fascinates me is a tangential issue. Branching from Seddon's 'not what they are called nor where they are found', I ask myself why it is we choose to name a plant what we do. A scientific system gives its own confirmations, but why do we 'nickname' and localise names?

Back to the trigger-words. As kids, we often called 'powder-barks' and 'wandoos' different names. There were good reasons for these misnamings, and in the same way that I have explored elsewhere the misnaming of birds (especially parrots), so I would like to explore the implications in this case.

In *The New Arcadia* – a long poem working through models of the epic – I have tried to explore tensions between the extremely local, even hermetic, and a broader historic and multi-geographical pastoral. The book is about a small part of Australia – the central wheatbelt of Western Australia – but even within this finite space, it is about specific roads, patches of land, peoples. Rumour and gossip are placed on the same footing, on an equal stage, with scientific fact and data, the mechanisms of farming, geology and geography. It's all in the eclogic mix. There are, hopefully, broader conversations at work – on micro and macro scales.

In theory, *The New Arcadia* collapses personal and related experience, and becomes a revivification of memory. I have travelled that road I mentioned my entire life, and know it extremely well. Recently, vandals have taken to painting 'smiley faces' on old-growth trees along the roadside there, in the national park. This has angered me deeply. I know trees individually. Around my uncle's farm Wheatlands, our usual destination, there used to be some majestic salmon gums on the gravel road above the salt wastes. Further up the higher ground, majestic stands of wandoo. As kids we called all pinkish-orange eucalypts salmon gums in celebration of these massive trees with their spreading canopies. The wandoo – also known as white gum, especially by farmers – had a rough mottled bark that literally looked spotted at times. 'Where are you kids going?' 'We're going up to the top bush to mess around in the spotted gums'. You get the idea.

Salmon gums generally grow in loamy soil. They are found on higher ground, but mainly on lower areas. Furthermore, you don't really start seeing them until you get to the other side of York, reaching their intensity out in the goldfields. Sadly, there are relatively few left, as the clearing of the wheatbelt has meant thin stands of trees persisting, and these often on slightly higher more marginal land. It gives a wrong impression of their preference, if you like. The trees I refer to as salmon gums at the beginning of *The New Arcadia* are those on the roadside near Wambyn Reserve – my cousin Ken, a tree expert, says it's possible salmon gums might be in the district around there but he hasn't seen them and confirms the trees visible from the Great Southern Highway are powderbarks and wandoos.

Wambyn is an indigenous name for the area. That area was once to be cleared but was put aside for local wood collecting until being made a nature reserve in 1970. Wambyn is only 215.2 hectares and in the entire York and Northam shire region only 0.6 percent of land has been put aside as flora and fauna reserve.

The Wambyn so-called 'salmon gums' glow orange, pink, and red at sunset, and are well known to those regularly driving the road. I heard a while back that someone has featured them in a major photo exhibition in the city. Opposite them are stands of wandoo ('white gums') climbing up through the rocky outcrops – our 'spotted gums'. The orange/pink/red trees are in reality powderbarks (*E. accedens*), with maybe the occasional orange-barked wandoo. There is also a so-called 'salmon bark wandoo', though I am not sure if these trees officially fit that category; probably this fed into our childhood conceptions and morphed into 'salmon gums' – we used to collect 'info' from all sorts of sources and come to our own conclusions. The unifying factor is that they are all eucalypts.

A frequently planted ornamental in the northern wet zone, particularly in Darwin, is *E. alba* – known as white gum, poplar gum, and... wait for it... 'salmon gum'. Here's part of the description from *A Gardener's Guide to Eucalypts* by Ivan Holliday and Geoffrey Watton (Hamlyn, Port Melbourne, repr. 1989): 'Bark is powdery white, but salmon pink when the old bark is first shed.' And:

> Occurrence: Widespread in the tropical north of Australia, from Western Australia across the 'Top End' to north Queensland, it is also one of the few eucalypts found naturally outside Australia – in Papua New Guinea, Java, Timor and other islands to the north. It can be found in thick stands inland and in places extends virtually to the sea.

> Cultivation: A useful ornament tree for the monsoonal areas, such as Darwin where it is cultivated as 'Salmon Gum'. Also a popular cultivated tree in other tropical countries such as Fiji. (1989, p. 30)

The salmon gum of the Western Australian wheatbelt and goldfields is a very different tree – thriving in low to moderate rainfall areas, and though being inclined towards loamy soil, growing in most soil types. Of this variety – *E. salmonophloia* – our guide says: 'The fresh bark is smooth and salmon or brownish orange, but it ages to pale grey with brown patches, shedding in flakes. The tree can be distinguished by its fresh bark and shining, dark green, lanceolate to falcate leaves' (1989, p. 230).

The spotted gum (*E. maculata*) is even more interesting in its versatility of name. Native to the east coast, it is only found in Western Australia in plantations, as part of bauxite rehabilitation programmes, and privately planted. It grows well in most places in Australia, though it does not like the very dry areas. It grows tall, and its bark is described thus: 'A feature is the mottled or spotted, clean grey-green or cream bark with dimpled dark grey patches' (1989, p. 160). It might sound similar to a description of a wandoo's bark, other than texture. One gathers the species got its scientific and (hence?) local name because of the way it looked. Talking to my brother about these issues, he says with a shearer's pragmatism: 'I've heard white gums called spotted gums all my life – who cares what it's really called? – it's what we know it by that matters…'

The process of naming is at the basis, as is frequently observed, of surveying, controlling, occupying land. Be it indigenous naming systems, or the colonising science of empire, the negotiation of space (clearly, to often very different ends) rests on identification within personal and common languages (oral, visual, written, performed and so on). This is simply restating what has been so often stated before. But particularly interesting to me are the idiosyncrasies of naming within small communities, in families, or by individuals. Giving something a pet name, for example. In utilising a pet name in a poem – say, calling the Sydney Harbour Bridge 'The Jump' (if you're interested, because a guy I drove with once sent his car airborne on the Bridge at about three in the morning), does it mean one needs to qualify for the reader, or in doing so is the hermetic self of the poem damaged or denuded? Does it matter? I feel it does. In some senses, an essay like this may become a paranoid validation of the seemingly gratuitous or solipsistic – but I think there are greater issues at stake.

Before leaving *A Gardener's Guide to Eucalypts*, I'll quote the entry for wandoo – it is very short, without its own page and tucked under 'Black Marlock'. As is shown, there's an instability about identifying the wandoo even within scientific nomenclature:

> *E. wandoo*: Blakely, Wandoo, is an erect, white-trunked tree of 30m high which bears similar flower buds and fruits. It has been considered a tree form of the Black Marlock, and was once known as *E. redunca var. elata*. It occurs in higher-rainfall areas (400-750 mm) of south-west Australia. (1989, p.216)

The hermetics of a poem are all very well if one wants to pursue sources, notes, conversations around the creation of a poem – the sort of readings that overwhelmingly enrich, say, a reading of Charles Olson's *Maximus Poems* – but most readers, of course, do not. Readers want to engage with a poem and have their experience within the poem, or at least within the book of poems. Readers expect to bring their own experience to that reading, and figurative language is rendered into a personal translation through analogy to personal observation, experience, reading, etc. Rarely, though, are readers bothered to go academic, and do the follow-ups. So, what does the poet wishing to communicate, and yet retain the hermetic, do?

One option is to indicate a consciousness of 'error' or 'wrong' in the systemics of the poem – in the expected knowledge of the poem. I have a strong fascination for environmental sciences, and pride myself on getting things 'right' in whichever terms I am using, or dealing with. So, clearly my best option would have been to include notes explaining what I was up to. For me, notes destroy poems. I could have alluded to an awareness of type/species identification issues by grammatical signage: the scare-quotes or italics or bolding of the words. Too intrusive. Too paranoid. The other approach is to give a hint within the flow of language – and that I did: 'from cryptic entanglements of salmon gums'. Cryptic insofar as it's a personal naming that creates an error zone – a place where the empirical folds into the imagined, where fact might seem fiction but is really an alternative measure of fact. The 'entanglements' are the necessary crossovers and overlays that come out of the personal growth of language – for writer and reader. We rethink received knowledge. The indigenous names of trees and places, the imposition of a scientific system on the entire world, the spatialities of animals and plants in their own terms – all are entangled, for good or bad.

The encryption is of name and reality, of description and identification. Full explication can only be received by reading the whole book and seeing that the geography and belonging are not delineated in this way elsewhere. The misnaming (or, I would argue, a naming every bit as legitimate) is a guide to dislocation, a guide to discomfort in belonging, especially given the intense local sense of connection being portrayed. Thus we begin with a Russellian paradox, but one that's axiomatically resolvable. 'The set of all sets that do not contain themselves as members' resolves itself in that the names of the trees are fluid, and they are neither part of and always part of any set at any given time. It is the same with the driveways and fencelines – the periphery of any drive we do not see or observe. What is being talked about could be off the beaten track, out of eyelines, and in the imagination. And the imagination is where poetry resides, though I am the first to say poetry is fact, not fiction – at least as I seek to write it. That paradox again.

Recalling names from childhood is a tricky business. Remember arguing over the words of a song lyric, and then going through most of your life before discovering that you were wrong all along, no matter how fiercely you defended your interpretation? (According to an episode of the music quiz show I have literally just been watching, this mishearing of music lyrics is called a 'Mondegreen' – the show delivers a 'misheard' line and the contestants have to come up with the correct name of the song! Ah, such is synchronicity... the *machine* in the *ghost*...) The internet resolves things quickly now – you can be guaranteed there are discussions and evidence concerning your obsession somewhere – yet it remains a truism. It is how we hear something that matters. For me, though I give way and utilise a recognised and comparatively common system of naming through the bulk of my work, the experientiality of first naming matters most. Interestingly, I would never call something 'salmon-coloured' now. When family called those trees 'salmon gums', it was because of the colour of salmon flesh – but I have been a vegan for most of my adult life and find different comparatives. And seeing spotted gums now, they are trees so different from our 'spotted gums' that the logic is diluted. Still, we had our reasons... and I have at least begun a book like that, without the scare-quotes, which, as will be evident by now, I find hard to do...

Note

If readers are interested, there is a lot of 'official'/government scientific information regarding the York and Northam nature reserves at the following website:
http://www.calm.wa.gov.au/national_parks/management/pdf_files/york_northam.pdf.
For all the utilitarianism, bureaucracy, and clinical tone, there are some quite poetic moments among the (interesting) facts there!

Two Poems by Alexander Heald

Oh Pretty Hedge

Oh pretty hedge that rustles by my house
Green parent of the hedgehog and the mouse
I shall destroy you with my power saw
Then build a concrete wall where you were growing.

Who needs another boring nature poem?
I'll cover you in blankets that I'll douse
With lighter fuel, then touch you with a match so you can roar.
And so, like butterflies inspired by your ire,

Thieving, sociopathic children jump your pyre
Aboard my neighbour's Piaggio, which they've stolen from his door.
Their immolation will, oh hedge, be such a pretty sight –
What poem could compete with kids alight?

Expatriates

We're all in countries we didn't create –
Of Roman floors and tans and tennis courts.
We're illegitimate, we're all expatriate.

We ate roast lamb beneath an olive's shade.
When asked, that's what I almost said. You've bought
A living in a country you didn't create.

Who hasn't moved? They thought we were dismayed
As real Brits, for whom the past was fought
And fight: legitimate, not them, expatriate

Of weather, government, whatever-gates.
They saw it on a map. Why were we sought
By this un-ending country? We didn't create

Its cityscapes and edges, crimes and greats,
Its language, or the stories we've been taught,
That make us patriots, and it legitimate.

We're just on journeys from and to our place,
Barges under cranes, sailors stopped at port.
Our countries leave us packed inside our crates.
Legitimate beneath expatriates.

In a Strange Land

Vicky Seal

There are ants on the tree, the children are screaming and she wishes it would rain.

Salej watches an ant reach a knobbly piece of bark, hesitate, rear up, then turn back. Where was it going in such a hurry, if turning back makes no difference?

Her dark eyes flicker out to where the children are playing. The bigger ones stand in groups, talking. It is the smaller ones, Salej's size, who run about shrieking to each other. She shrinks behind her tree. If it rains all the children will go into the big building.

And then what?

Mother brought her very early. She had the twins with her to take to somewhere else.

'You have to stay here until I come for you, Salej. I am busy with your Aunt Shamil. It is the law that you come here. Do not cry.'

Salej sniffs. Does it matter to cry if there is no one to see you? Mother had not said. Salej thinks not, and here are cold tears on her lower lids. When she thinks of Mother's voice they get bigger until they roll out.

Earlier they sat in the dark room behind Aunt Shamil's shop. Mother gave Salej a cup of strong coffee and a sweet roll. Aunt Shamil said: 'Poor little thing! At least the twins have each other.'

Mother replied: 'She must go.'

'Yes,' Aunt Shamil said. 'Poor little lamb.'

There is a sound like a musical instrument played on one note: bong bong bong bong bong! The children go to the building. The bigger ones walk, still chattering, and the smaller ones – Salej's size – skip or run.

Mother had pointed to the big building and said: 'In there. I will be here again when it is time.' And now the children are hurrying up the steps. Salej wipes her eyes and follows.

'Ah, Sally! Come with me!' A woman at the steps takes Salej's hand and leads her inside. She is talking all the while but Salej cannot answer. The woman opens a door just inside the entrance and shows

Salej there are toilets. Salej nods, not meeting the woman's eyes.

They go to another room where children are seated at rows of desks. There is a beautiful lady at the front of the room, wearing a blue dress. The two women talk briefly and the younger one smiles at Salej. Salej drops her eyes. The other woman leaves.

'Class, this is Sally al-Shatri.'

The children chorus: 'Hello, Sally!' Salej studies her sandals through a blur of tears.

The teacher smiles at Salej again and indicates a vacant desk. Salej sits, and stares straight ahead. Some of the children laugh. The teacher says something. The girl beside Salej takes the shopping bag containing Salej's lunch to the window side of the room, where a row of pegs supports a row of identical blue and yellow bags. Salej's plastic bag with the incomprehensible red lettering gleams like a beacon to her shame. The other girl sits again, smirking.

At an order from the teacher the children open their desks. It is a signal to talk, evidently. Salej's seat-mate addresses her in friendly tones as she removes an orange-covered book from the neat piles within. Salej says nothing; she sees that all the other children have orange books, too. She lifts the lid of her desk and finds there is nothing inside but a dirty, chipped ruler.

The lids are all shut with a clatter and one word from the teacher stops the class talking. The teacher says something about 'Sally' and her seat-mate pushes the book to the centre of their desks. The book is open. At the top is big writing, and a picture of a dog sitting by a chair. In the chair is an old woman, knitting. There is smaller writing under the picture.

The teacher talks. Some of the children raise their hands. The teacher nods, and a voice from the back begins to speak. Salej twists around, surprised, to see who is talking so long. No one seems to have noticed; all eyes are on their books.

Salej looks at the picture again, but before long she steals surreptitious glances around the room. Most of the other children are wearing blue jackets, each with a blue and yellow insignia on the top pocket. The boys have pale blue shirts, ties with thin yellow stripes, and dark grey trousers. The girls have blue dresses, and a few are wearing blue jumpers instead of jackets. Salej sees how the collars peep out of the neckline, which is edged in yellow. They all have grey socks and black shoes.

Salej has a sand-coloured shift dress and leather sandals. She is suddenly appalled at her own thin arms and legs, the colour of milky coffee. She wishes she could hide.

At break she walks to her tree. She walks slowly so no one will notice her. The ants have a dead moth which they are carrying up the tree.

Her mother said: 'Father has been killed. We must go to live with his rich sister.'

'Where?' Salej asked.

'Shamil lives in England. She has her own shop. She is very fat now and never goes hungry.'

'But where is Father?'

'He was killed in the desert. They buried him in the sand.'

'How can you be sure?'

'You must help me with the twins now, Salej.'

At night Salej thought of Father. He had been gone a long while, but one day he would come home. He would have jewellery for Mother, sweet things for the twins, a pet lizard for Salej.

The day they left, everyone cried but Salej. She told her friend Cedra: 'When Father comes, tell him we are gone to live with Aunt Shamil in her shop in England. Give him this scarf of mine.'

Cedra nodded, wide eyed, and promised.

Salej watches the other children. Two of the bigger girls are turning a rope while others run in and jump over it. They are all chanting something. If Cedra were with her they would join in. Cedra was never shy. With Cedra, Salej knew how to play, too.

Mother is waiting just outside the gate.

'Everyone comes but Salej! I thought you were lost.'

'I am here now.'

'We must hurry. The shop is very busy.'

'Where are the twins?'

'Pff! They are already home one hour. More. Notice which way we walk, Salej. Tomorrow you must come alone.'

'Why must I come? No one talks to me.'

'To learn English you must listen first. Use your ears and repeat what others say.'

'Quiet!' roars Salej.

'What is that?'

'It means the children must stop talking. The teacher says it when we open and close our special tables.' Mother is puzzled, so Salej adds: 'The table has a lid, and inside are books and pens.'

'Do you speak when you open your magic table?'

'Of course not,' Salej answers hotly. 'I have nothing to say. And then, I never open my table. There is nothing in mine.'

'Pff!' Mother says. 'You must do as the instructor tells you.'

They have reached the shop. Aunt Shamil is weighing beans into a paper sack and there are customers waiting. Mother waves Salej through to the back.

The twins are in great high spirits under the friendly incandescent light globe, hiding behind sacks and boxes, leaping out to shoot each other with invisible but noisy guns. Salej sits gingerly on her fold-up camp bed and for a long time they continue their game, ignoring her and making the dust fly. Finally one of them runs along the narrow path between the teetering plastic crates and Salej's bed. She grabs the wriggling, red-faced tot. It is Pala. Once she is silenced, Eliph emerges from a dim corner.

'What did you do today?' Salej asks. 'Did you play?'

Both twins nod emphatically. How they played! First they painted pictures with lovely bright paints on big sheets of paper. The paper was as white as their walls at home had been, with no wood in it. Then they joined hands with all the other children and skipped in a circle while the teacher played piano. They all sang a song.

'Wait!' says Salej. 'Did you sing, too?'

Oh yes, the twins say. Eliph was shouting: 'You all have feet like camels, your faces are like sheep, you chatter like the monkeys…' So Pala sang Eliph's song, too, and the other children were so puzzled! Then after that they all sat in a circle and the teacher showed cards. There was a picture of a tree and all the children yelled 'Tree!' while the teacher pointed to letters on the card, 'Door!' 'Box!' 'Dog!' Pala remembers all the words and shows Salej what a 'Box!' is, then a 'Door!'

Eliph wants to talk about the teacher reading from a book while all the children lay on mats on the floor. She had been so bored, and then when all the children sat up she realised Pala had fallen asleep. Everyone had laughed, even the teacher.

Pala giggles. Salej smiles, too.

Aunt Shamil has closed the shop and they assemble at the kitchen table, the two women and three girls. There is bread, two kinds of beans, some tough meat and goat cheese. Mother and Aunt Shamil drink red wine from a big bottle. Over Mother's protests, Aunt Shamil pours a little wine for Salej, too.

'She needs it,' Aunt Shamil says. 'See how pale…! It will put vigour in her blood.'

Salej takes a sip. The wine tastes sour but she sips again until it is all gone. Then Mother takes the twins upstairs. They are sleeping one each end of the big couch in the room overlooking the street. Salej helps Aunt Shamil with the dishes.

'I expect you are tired,' Aunt Shamil says.

'I am.'

'All day people speaking English around you. You will learn to speak it, too, Salej, and then you will be very happy here.'

'No,' says Salej, thinking: Father will take us home again. He promised me a lizard with eyes like topaz.

Aunt Shamil is feigning interest in a baked-on stain. 'Your mother says you did not cry for my poor murdered brother. It is better to cry, little one, or the tears will turn into stones inside you.'

Salej dries the cup from which she drank her first wine, and says nothing.

'Both are asleep,' Mother says, coming in. 'Here, Salej, let me finish that. It has been a hard day for you.'

Salej nods and gives up the tea towel. But later, when the two women have gone up to share Aunt Shamil's big bed, she lies wakeful. Learn English. Learn English. Aunt Shamil speaks English all day to her customers. The twins already have several words. The hairs all over her head stand up and there is a feeling like ice in her stomach. Father is dead. Father is dead and lying under the sand. They will never leave this cold, drab place. She will not see her friend Cedra again. Everyone will speak English except Salej. And Father. . .

She puts her hands over her face and sobs.

In the morning she refuses to eat breakfast.

'What?' asks Mother. 'You must eat. And if you do not eat you must still go to the school.'

'I will go.'

Aunt Shamil puts Salej's breakfast in the shopping bag with her lunch. 'Eat when you are ready,' she says kindly. 'Today will be better than yesterday. And tomorrow will be better again.'

Salej walks to school swinging the bag. Even now she is the smallest in her class, and very thin. If she did not eat, in three days she would be a skeleton. Then she would be with Father.

The children are playing and shouting. Salej watches from behind her tree. There are no ants this morning. Where have they gone?

She enters the school with the others, finds her room, hangs her plastic bag on a peg.

'Hello Sally!' calls the teacher – and a question. Salej glances at her, her mouth set. The teacher looks troubled. Salej takes her seat.

'Hello Sally,' says her seat-mate.

The children open their desks. Under the general commotion Salej mutters: 'Hello Sally' and 'Quiet!' Her seat-mate indicates that she should open her desk. Salej lifts the lid. There are books and pens inside! The other girl selects two books and a pen, and slaps them on top. She shows Salej that the thinner book is full of white paper ruled with blue lines.

Salej studies the first page. The twins spoke the truth: the paper is white like the clouds, with no splinters. While the other children frown over the text books and write in their exercise books, Salej uses the chipped ruler to draw lines down the page. Soon she has a whole page of squares.

At an order from the teacher the children put their books away, then they carry their chairs to the front of the room and form a half-circle. The teacher sets up a white board and begins to write on it with a red pen. Questions are asked, and answers given. Then the teacher drops her pen. The pen jumps up once and rolls near to Salej.

Salej bends to pick up the pen and freezes, arm outstretched. No one else has moved. She looks up to the teacher. The teacher is smiling and nodding. Salej drops her eyes, retrieves the pen, and gives it to the teacher.

'Thank you, Sally!'

Salej sits back. Thank you, Sally. Thank you means: 'I am grateful.' It means: 'You have done something good.'

Salej whispers: 'Thank you, Sally.'

At break time she takes her breakfast roll to the playground and sits on a bench. She begins to eat so she will not become a skeleton. She listens to the skipping girls' chant.

'Hi, Sally.' It is her seat-mate in the classroom. The girl sits beside Salej and talks to her. Salej says nothing, watching the moving lips, hearing the unfathomable sounds as she continues to eat her roll.

The girl points to her and says: 'Sally.' She points to herself and says: 'Gina.'

Salej nods. She swallows the last of her roll and says: 'Gina.'

'You got it!'

Salej points to herself and says: 'Salej.'

Gina's eyes widen. 'Sulledge?'

Salej nods again. It is close enough.

Two Poems by Neil Curry

At Le Café de la Gare

The table they'd been shown to was so small
They could have easily reached out to slap
Each other across the face, had they had

A mind to. At least they were in the shade
Now, out of the glare of alternatives.
Weighed down by leisure, they sat and waited.

Rehearsed, 'S'îl vous plait, un mille feuille
And deux tasses de thé.' The silence bulged,
But failed to burst. It was as if all this

Had taken place a year or more ago
And only through some glitch of memory
Was of concern to them. And there were still

The qualms of the evening to be got through yet.

Other Rooms

Afterwards, all he could remember clearly
Was the sound that the rain made, splattering
Against the paper wrappers of the flowers

Someone had been arranging around her grave.
He turned away from the window. When people
Are always there one tends to forget them.

And moved a cushion, but did not sit.
To be *gone*, a person needs to have been,
To be somebody something had once happened to.

He thought perhaps to make some tea. When
There is not love enough to go around,
It ought to be the dead who go without.

Another room, another frontier. There would
Be others: stairs and doors. He could
Recall their bodies' fond acquaintanceship.

These were her gloves. Something akin,
He guessed, to immortality lay in his longing.
Elsewhere would be her shoes, and other things.

A Shed of One's Own

Chris Routledge

In July 2003 I began building a writing hut; the idea had been brewing for a while. Working at home is fine until the doorbell rings, or the window cleaner calls, or you have people to stay and there is work to be done and nowhere to do it. As Virginia Woolf noted in 1929, a busy household full of visitors, children, and other distractions is no place for a writer. There was also the issue of the garden, which was starting to draw me outside more and more often. A few years before we had seeded it with native British wild flowers, so in the summer months it was a mass of campion and daisies and trefoils and a hundred other things. But even in the winter there were things to look at: an early daffodil shoot pushing up through dead leaves, a bird hunting for food.

I worked on the writing hut between July and October in the evenings, at weekends, and any spare days I could find. I was engrossed in calculations of the lengths of wood needed for each stage, the amount of pitch a roof needs to shed water, and how window frames are made. On holiday in Scotland that year I took notes on the construction of the roofs of crofts and worried that mine was built too light. And then there was the language. I learned to use phrases like 'collar ties' (the cross-beams that hold roof trusses together), 'studs and cats' (the vertical and horizontal beams in the walls), 'soles and top plates' (the beams running along the top and bottom of a stud wall), shingles and eaves. During the day I was editing a book on the philosophy of language; I hammered and sawed until dusk.

By October it was finished and I started writing at the bottom of the garden in November. I still don't quite know what it was that made me do it. The work was physically and mentally hard, but deeply rewarding. That first week, listening to the Lancashire rain pounding on the roof I made, and not coming in, I felt connected with something very old and very human. That feeling is also there in the process of writing itself. There is the construction, collecting materials and shaping them into something new, but there is also something more elemental: the need for shelter and to communicate are part of what we are. Perhaps for that reason writers have always been escape artists, constantly seeking a place where they can connect at a deep level with the world outside. For many that has meant running away to cabins in the woods, distant islands, and garden sheds. For others, like the American writer John Cheever, a windowless basement was enough. Every morning Cheever took the elevator down from his New York apartment block and worked on a bare wooden table facing a blank wall.

Some writers are very specific about the environment they can work in and go to great lengths to avoid working anywhere else. This was a particular problem in Hollywood in the 1930s and 1940s, where even well-known writers were forced to work in shared offices, producing work to order. Raymond Chandler had an especially bad experience working with Billy Wilder on *Double Indemnity* (1944). He didn't like Wilder's pacing up and down, his taking phone calls from women, or the fact that he wore his hat in the office and waved a baton around. Luckily Chandler was famous enough and valuable enough to the studio to wring an apology from the notoriously arrogant director.

Having learned his lesson, Chandler's demands for finishing *The Blue Dahlia* (1946) were more exacting: if he was going to write for Hollywood, he would do it on his own terms and in a place where he was comfortable. In his case that was at home in La Jolla, with a supply of whiskey and coffee, round-the-clock secretaries to type up his dictation, and a fleet of limousines to ferry the script to the studio page by page as it was finished. Even so the arrangement nearly killed him and Chandler said of his experience: 'I was convinced in the beginning that there must be some discoverable method of working in pictures which would not be completely stultifying to whatever creative talent one might happen to possess. But like others before me I discovered that this was a dream.'[1]

One of those others was William Faulkner, who in the 1930s became well known for his successful escape attempts and did most of his work from home in Oxford, Mississippi despite the complaints from studio bosses. But being quirky and rebellious costs money and by 1941 Faulkner was desperate and broke. The regular paid work was all that mattered and he was signed up to Warner Brothers for seven years at $300 a week, less than half his salary with MGM five years before. He wrote scripts for such classic movies as *To Have and Have Not* (1944) and *The Big Sleep* (1946), and contributed uncredited hack work to many others, including *Mildred Pierce* (1945). But the contrast between what he was doing and what he actually was is rather sad. In 1948 Faulkner did uncredited 'script doctor' work on a B-movie, *Adventures of Don Juan*; the following year he won the Nobel Prize for literature.

Hollywood during its golden age was a difficult place for writers, but the need for solitude and retreat has always been a high priority. So much so in fact that some writers have become famous for their quirky writing arrangements and in particular for working in garden sheds. George Bernard Shaw had a wooden studio built in the grounds of his house which rotated to follow the path of the sun, while Roald Dahl's tiny garden shed stood at the end of a small avenue of pleached lime trees and was notoriously spartan and uncomfortable. More recently Philip Pullman, author of the *His Dark Materials* trilogy, has been 'outed' as a garden shed writer, though since moving house he has donated his shed to a friend and moved indoors to a large study. Even so he claims to share his study with woodworking tools, so it remains a shed in spirit at least.

Mark Twain, who seems to have lived and worked in more Western towns than it is possible to visit in a lifetime, returned in the end to Elmira, New York, where his sister-in-law had built an octagonal cabin for him and which he later described as 'a cozy nest.' But in the nineteenth century it was much more unusual for writers to have a separate place for writing than it is now. William Wordsworth, who did much of his composing while he walked on the Lake District fells, also managed somehow to write at home. In the second volume of his biography of Samuel Taylor Coleridge, Richard Holmes describes the domestic hubbub that attended Coleridge's arrival at Allan Bank, Grasmere, where Wordsworth lived with his wife Mary, their three children, his sister Dorothy, and an assortment of animals:

> Domestic matters quickly engulfed [Coleridge]. Mary Wordsworth was about to give birth to her fourth child, rooms were still being decorated, De Quincey was expected, the Coleridge children were longing to see their father.[2]

Some more recent writers, including J. K. Rowling, and Ernest Hemingway, have been able to work in noisy environments such as cafés and bars, perhaps like Wordsworth being able to escape to a virtual space of their own, but for most the idea of existing in close proximity to so many people and still being able to write is almost inconceivable: later in life even Hemingway had a wooden cabin where he did his writing. But the guru of all shed-dwelling writers from Shaw to Dylan Thomas is Henry David Thoreau, who moved into his cabin in the forest near Concord, Massachusetts on July 4, 1845.

The cabin had taken Thoreau two months to build and his experiences there would become the subject of his best-known work, *Walden*, a book with which he established himself as an observer of nature and as one of America's great transcendentalist writers. Thoreau's book is a celebration of the solitude he enjoyed in the woods and while his move began as an experiment in living without the comforts of modern life, Thoreau's reasons for going there are more writerly than scientific: 'I went to the woods,' he says, 'because I wished to live deliberately'.[3] What he meant was partly to discover what it was like to live outside what he saw as the over-regulated, consumerist society of Concord, but he was also talking about the writing process itself. Thoreau's need to 'front only the essential facts of life,' and to do so in solitude, is one that most writers will recognise.

Over the following decades *Walden* was hugely successful. It seemed to touch on something in the American psyche that craved a reconnection with what F. Scott Fitzgerald in *The Great Gatsby* (1926) called 'a fresh, green breast of the new world'. In the 1960s and 1970s *Walden* inspired a generation of hippies, drop-outs, and environmentalists to shun the materialism of their time, just as Thoreau had done for his own. But Thoreau's retreat to the woods was driven only in part by a desire to escape from everyday life and live more simply: he also wanted a place to work. In the two years he lived in his cabin Thoreau not only maintained a journal that he would later write up as *Walden*, but he wrote his first book, *A Week on the Concord and Merrimack Rivers* (1849). His cabin is a prototype to which writers have turned ever since.

Walden is full of detail about Thoreau's life in the woods – the minutiae of his success growing vegetables, a description of tiny silver fish in the pond, how he cooked his food – yet what we learn from the book is as much about the life Thoreau left behind in town as it is about life in the woods. Thoreau's distance from everyday life made him a useful and passionate social critic. In the suburbanised, information-driven twentieth century, where travel became very easy, the kind of escape Thoreau achieved gradually became more difficult, yet for many writers the need for retreat and reflection became more urgent. A dramatic example of this need to 'live deliberately' is provided by George Orwell, who in May 1946 moved into a farmhouse called Barnhill at the northern tip of the island of Jura, off the west coast of Scotland. Following the death of his wife Eileen in 1945 Orwell hoped to make a permanent home there for himself and his son, Richard, but in the short term he was also looking for a place to write the novel that would become *1984*.

Jura is a dramatic, beautiful, and savage place. Looking east in good weather from Barnhill you can see in the distance the low jagged shadow of the Scottish coast; to the north the treacherous Corryvreckan whirlpool and the tiny island of Sarba. Jura is small, just 24 miles long, with a single narrow road running north from the jetty at the southern end along the eastern coast. In Orwell's time the road ran for only 17 miles of the island's length, so from the hamlet of Ardlussa where it ended he had a seven-mile walk home along a rough track. Suffering from the early effects of the tuberculosis that eventually killed him, Orwell often took to his bed and worked on the novel there, but when he felt well he took long walks on the empty hills. A setting more removed from the dystopian urban nightmare of Orwell's best-known novel is difficult to imagine. I spent a few days near Barnhill in the late 1980s, sheltering from a violent, days-long storm in a tiny tent, and have never felt so untied from the modern world as then.

Orwell died in 1950 and the manuscript of *1984* was discovered at Barnhill some time later. Clearly Jura suited him, but for most writers solitude needs to be found closer to friends, relatives, and ordinary life. My own writing hut, nestled at the bottom of the garden and surrounded with wild flowers, has become a favourite place. In the spring and summer there is birdsong and the hum of insects; in the winter there is wind and rain to accompany the work. Thoreau catches exactly the feeling of having found a place to write: 'I think that the richest vein is somewhere hereabouts; so by the divining rod and thin rising vapor I judge; and here I will begin to mine.'[4]

1 Letter to Hamish Hamilton, November 10, 1950. In Frank MacShane (ed.), *The Selected Letters of Raymond Chandler*, New York: Dell, 1987, p. 237.

2 Holmes, Richard, *Coleridge: Darker Reflections*, HarperCollins, 1998, pp. 146–47.

3 Thoreau, Henry David, *Walden* (1854). This edition, Penguin, 1983, p. 135.

4 *Walden*, p. 143.

Two Poems by Pamela Lewis

Reading Group

Three women converge in a corner,
raise curiosity over the coffee,
late middle-aged and middle-class.

They have discovered mutual pain,
recognition is enough, mild comfort,
almost laugh about parallel lives.

Small cars wait outside on the hill,
short walks too much in the winter,
pretend laziness as a thin excuse.

We have adapted like animals
to our prevailing condition,
fly and crawl from day to day.

Easy to understand the genre,
reading the signs as sentences,
we read each other like a book.

Two Lines

Everything goes on,
sometimes I join in,
usually I travel
in parallel.

Wild Analysis

Michael Murphy

I spent the winter and spring of 2005 as Writer-in-Residence at the National Wildflower Centre, based in Knowsley's Court Hey Park. The residency was made possible by a grant from the Arts Council of England. The brief I gave myself was to study and write about ways in which human patterns of migration have affected the dispersal of flora. It was a theme that tied in with a number of poems from my first full collection, *Elsewhere*, in which, as well as the metaphorical sense in which to write, to enter the imaginary, is to find oneself, for good and bad, transported to a place that is neither here nor there but elsewhere, I also wrote about exile as it affects individuals and a city such as Liverpool.

I grew up within a stone's throw of Court Hey Park, and so my memories of the place tap into both personal experience and historical events. For example, on the edges of the park, where there is now a housing estate, there used to be offices run by Vernon's Pools. Outside the offices were a number of grassed-over air-raid shelters. As kids we used to slip in through holes in the wire fence and play soldiers on these mounds. I remember how I used to wear a navy blue zip-up jacket. Stitched onto it were the wings of the Parachute Regiment in which my father did his National Service. Even then I had some vague sense that the bunkers on which we played weren't empty, that they still contained bodies dormant like seeds, waiting for a change in the weather, the all-clear.

My residency coincided with the sixtieth anniversary of VE Day. Sixty years ago the shattered populations of Europe marked in their various ways the end of the Second World War. While some danced in the streets, others were too exhausted to summon the spirit. For large parts of the continent the end of war meant the beginning of a hard, steady climb back to affluence and influence; for millions more it meant a descent akin to Persephone's into the Inferno of the Soviet Union. Oblivious to, though not unaffected by, Europe's attempt at obliterating itself, nature carried on regardless. Such a perspective fed into a sequence of thirty 'Essays' written for the thirtieth birthday of Landlife, a charity committed to establishing new environments for wildflowers in both urban and rural areas, fostering sustainability and biodiversity. *Landlife* first put down roots in Liverpool's Lark Lane in 1975, and it is to its tenacious efforts that we owe the resource and inspiration that is the National Wildflower Centre.

A starting point for the sequence was a French term for wildflowers, *les fleurs mauvaises*. The phrase attracted me because of the amount of spleen and invective it contains. *Bad, wrong, jaundiced, feeble, perverse, defective, lousy, immoral, insincere...* Perhaps what riles us about *les fleurs mauvaises* is that a wild flower exists beyond censure, and this makes us want to turn it into a scapegoat for human ills. The wildflower's is a life of oblivious and obvious excess. It exists only to flower and to produce more of the same. Which reminds me of what I think is Umberto Eco's definition of a writer: a trick pulled off by books to produce another book.

Originally a *verse* was the point at which a plough turns as it moves from one end of a field to the other. A poem, then, breaks open the unfurrowed material of the unconscious, keeling it over, oxygenating, allowing new material to emerge. As culture, all art articulates the space between Self and World. It is, in essence, a process whereby the wild is grafted to civilisation. So I decided to bed what I experienced in the octosyllabic couplet. What I had in mind was a poet such as Marvell, for whom nature is closely allied with human consciousness ('My Mind was once the true survey / Of all these Medows fresh and gay'), or the radically different vision of Blake's 'Auguries of Innocence'. Metrically, however, I cut myself some slack, as does Pope in his 'An Essay on Man' (an ironic rejoinder to which is provided by the title of my own sequence), where the addition of an extra foot enacts his vision of nature as 'A wild, where weeds and flowers promiscuous shoot'. A final influence was Voltaire's *Candide*, the final words of which are 'We must cultivate our garden'. Candide says this after he and his companions have experienced the worst nature can throw at them. They retreat from Europe to establish a second Eden on the banks of the Bosphorus, an Eden where they are made to work for their livelihood and where fruitless speculation, philosophising, is banned. Yet how long would it have taken Candide to reach a position where he felt secure enough to sow wildflowers instead of utilitarian herbs and vegetables? When could he afford to take time off to read and write, and when would it again be safe to approach and take responsibility for eating from the Tree of Knowledge? Only then, it seems to me, when he could allow the wild to co-exist with the cultivated, would Candide be able to say he was civilised. For it is the highest mark of civilisation to allow those things which trouble and disturb us to have their say. As Gerard Manley Hopkins wrote, 'Let them be left, / O let them be left, wildness and wet; / Long live the weeds and the wilderness yet.'

A Poem by
Michael Murphy

Essays

The angel glowering at the gate
Of Eden, anticipates
les fleurs mauvaises

Birdsong. Silence congregates
In even the meanest sink estate
les fleurs mauvaises

Bishops know, like Crazy Jane,
Souldiers Cullions aren't to blame
les fleurs mauvaises

Bittercress. Its compact pinnate
Leaves a famine ship under sail
les fleurs mauvaises

A blue tit in the nest box lays
Eleven eggs. Magpies count the days
les fleurs mauvaises

Bramble bushes planted on graves
Teach sheep where they may safely graze
les fleurs mauvaises

A calyx rattles. You hear feet
On a forced march. A meadow migrates
les fleurs mauvaises

The cornflower is articulate
On matters other than love and hate
les fleurs mauvaises

Dido's lament, Forget-me-not,
Sings the blues above a backyard gate
les fleurs mauvaises

For a moment, then, I saw Christ sway-
ing on the crossbeams of Spiked May
les fleurs mauvaises

The green fuse in the earth ignites
A winter sun. Pluto's aconite
les fleurs mauvaises

Harvest. Grass lies down to the blade
As Persephone's skirts are raised
les fleurs mauvaises

Hitler was intoxicated
By Valerian's whiff of sweat
les fleurs mauvaises

In a time of dearth, calculate
Love like a seed's atomic weight
les fleurs mauvaises

Just for once, take a minute
To watch grass bend first this way then that
les fleurs mauvaises

The kissing season. Gorse fires are lit.
Seeds crack open in the heat
les fleurs mauvaises

Like the skins of bruised fruits –
Poems crushed under a critic's boots
les fleurs mauvaises

Metaphors? Vacuum-sealed horse shit
For all history can't accommodate
les fleurs mauvaises

The migrant dead, poppy's rash blaze
Cast shadows in the summer haze
les fleurs mauvaises

On ring roads, down blind alleyways,
Last year's fallen rise with heads ablaze
les fleurs mauvaises

A rift in clouds. Sunlight. Let us pray.
Bluebells bow their heads in conclave
les fleurs mauvaises

Spring like the H-bomb detonates
Angels pirouetting on mass graves
les fleurs mauvaises

A sweet disorder? Herbicide
Puts wanton Herrick in the shade
les fleurs mauvaises

Sunlight turns shadows into faces
Of the dead. Dried flower bouquets
les fleurs mauvaises

Voltaire counselled: >>Cultivate
Your garden.<< Wipe clean the slate
les fleurs mauvaises

Washed, chopped and mixed with suet,
Sliced and fried in rich pork fat
les fleurs mauvaises

A watering can of Glysophate
Predicts the ruin of the state
les fleurs mauvaises

Where its sowing is deliberate
Kiss-me-quick unlocks the heart
les fleurs mauvaises

Wordless. Fallible. Commensurate
With all we thought to forget
les fleurs mauvaises

You can't interpret, little less translate
All the hawthorn predicates
les fleurs mauvaises

The Practice of Poetry

Images and Names in Susan Wicks's 'Vocabulary'

Adam Piette

The making of poems feels like a solemn and primitive activity because there is still a sense in which it harks back to the original naming of objects and creatures in mankind's earliest acts of speech. Many theories of language development imagined the first speakers to be magical poets in Elysian fields giving names to the plants and animals – Adam in Eden, Orpheus with his lyre, Virgil's shepherd-poets and their flocks. And just as poetry summons up the earliest encounters of humans with other life forms, so each individual in their lifetime moves from strange elemental meetings with the natural world in childhood, through language learning, towards a 'fallen' knowledge of the world. Something of this double process is running through Susan Wicks's poem 'Vocabulary':

Vocabulary

These flora and fauna have no names:
crimson-bodied, orange-throated,
black-gold mosaic-winged,
straight-stemmed, shrill-voiced,
they mass in skeins, packs, shoals,
howl through dark or flash silver,
bending, beating, reflected in still water.
Later I learn them from books:
cardinal, Indian paintbrush, coyote –
match each with an image and mount it
in sequence on blank paper: cholinesterase,
multiple sclerosis, poison oak.

The poem seems simple, its structure a two-sentence argument of innocence and experience. But in its detail, the poem is surprisingly difficult to prise open. Something about those colons makes the poem read too easily as a demonstration – *here* are some of the flora and fauna. But the demonstrative gesture fails to match up quite with the presented evidence. The first set of flora and fauna are given us as plural, but it is impossible not to try and bundle the features up into a specific genus or species. Trying to imagine a creature with the features listed in lines 2 to 6 produces a frightening, surreal image, like some monster out of Dr Seuss. No wonder the creature cannot be named – it must come from the dark unconscious of children's unspeakable nightmares.

At the same time, logic prevails and we can work some form of rational code out of the list: Wicks is naming the abstract features of a variety of different flora and fauna – flowers, birds, butterflies, wolves, fish – in a bewildering succession of flashes and visions, bursts of action and gesture from the animal and plant world, like quarks of elemental energy. This intermittent power is mimicked by the verbal force of Wicks's adjectives (the insistent four-beat rhythm helps with this). Not being able to name what is being seen gives the phenomena this strange alien beat, an inscape effect almost.

It is also the namelessness which adds sinister edge to the ways the flora and fauna mass together to the primordial poet's mind. Those three great lines – 'they mass in skeins, packs, shoals, / howl through dark or flash silver, / bending, beating, reflected in still water' – are thick with compacted forces (mimed in the compacted sound-repetitions), forming a locally conflicted zone of archetypal intensities at the heart of the poem. The words seethe with the energies borrowed from the natural world so fiercely imagined by the dreaming mind. If poetry has an originating crucible, Wicks is arguing, it must be here in the massed and beating animal/plant-life visions of our earliest years; as reflected in the 'still water' of the child's reverie, captured as still words on the page.

This queer mystery – that the original namelessness of natural phenomena may be the source of poetry – is partly resolved, the poem is saying in its own cryptic way, if one accepts the argument that poetry is *first and foremost* a matter of energies and forces and beats. It is also of course a matter of images – the *imagistes* at least got that right. The poet's basic repertoire is made up of a host of thronging images in the mind's museum of memory and imagination. That they are *bodied, throated* and *voiced*, as Wicks insists, is a measure of the ways the imagination sees them first, as already incorporated as potential energies within the poet's own scribal and singing system, her body, throat and voice.

The move to names, for Wicks, is not necessarily a fall into an alien system, for what is read includes the flora and fauna of the world never experienced. The three examples of cardinal, Indian paintbrush, coyote are all American, implying a new set of images for the English poet. Nevertheless, something of the predatoriness of the natural world carries over from the line 'they mass in skeins, packs, shoals' (so close to 'they *hunt* in skeins, packs, shoals'). At some considerable risk of overreading, the red cardinal bird and red (and parasitic) paintbrush flower collocate bloodily with the pack-hunting coyote.

What is suddenly shocking and so disruptive of the Wordsworthian-Hopkinsian-Lawrentian complex Wicks' poem seemed to be constructing is the third and final list of names after the second colon of the second sentence. The very fact there are two colons is striking, as though the poet were losing grip on the rationalising scape of her own poem (the sentence breaking up under some form of extreme pressure). But it is the list itself which breaks the poem apart: 'cholinesterase, /multiple sclerosis, poison oak.' Only poison oak preserves the flora-fauna theme in any recognisable way, just as it supplements the American list. But cholinesterase? Multiple sclerosis?

It is at this great faultline in this brief poem that life (and the threat of death) breaks in to the closed circle of the poem on the page. Readers need to know several things about Susan Wicks, and about the poem's contexts. First, that Susan Wicks was diagnosed with multiple sclerosis in the early 1990s, receiving the news at roughly the same time as she was discovering America as traveller and teacher of creative writing. Secondly, that Wicks's poems had been both celebrated and snubbed, according to point of view, as being focused on the domestic scene, the intimate relationship, the interiority of the woman's body. And thirdly, that the collection in which this poem appears, *Open Diagnosis*, has a whole central section of MS poems – 'Vocabulary', in other words, is part of a sequence of painful texts about the shock of living with the idea of the disease within (the word 'sequence' is in the poem to remind us of this). Fourthly, that MS is an autoimmune disease, the body attacking itself, specifically the myelin layer of tissue linking nerves, mistaken for virus. (Instead of normal antibodies, the body produces what are called *autoantibodies*, because they attack antigens that belong to the body's own self.) Lastly, cholinesterase is a complex enzyme which hoovers up unused neurotransmitters in the brain – multiple sclerosis patients are sometimes prescribed cholinesterase inhibitors which mean the neurotransmitters last longer, thus improving brain function. One of the debilitating symptoms of MS for a writer and teacher is the slurring of speech and confusion of ideas caused by the paralysing of nerve fibre.

To someone who knows all this, and in much greater detail since she had to learn all there is about the disease, to read all the books, such knowledge is immediately contagious, taken like an infectious oil deep into the skin, as with poison oak. Such knowledge links up with the extraordinary process of learning about the world's flora and fauna that the first two thirds of the poem are about. It joins that great chain back both to Susan Wicks's earliest childhood and to the earliest encounters of humans and other lifeforms because enzymes and autoantibodies are also forms of life, and they carry with them the potential to strike terror in the mind and body under threat, like the massed animal and plant energies of our species' archetypal experiences, like the ancient fears of biting, stinging, killing predators still operative even in the vocabulary of dangerous creatures and plants.

Cholinesterase and the MS lymphocytes may be invisible, locked away in vanishingly small pockets of blood supply and nerve fibre. Yet they yield a terrifying power to destroy the body, to act like predatory animals within our own animal bodies. And they *are* tiny Dr Seuss monsters, as strange as anything in the universe if seen as 3-D molecular models. The poetry they produce may be 'sick', as they say, but not only is that partly the point, but also suggests something further. To pronounce those three names, 'cholinesterase, /multiple sclerosis, poison oak', curling them across the line-ending like that, hearing the massed sound-repetitions (k, s, z, t, l), the sheer beauty of the diphthong modulation (-ase, -os-, -ois-), the rising rhythm surging up three times to the ends of the names, is to match images to names in a very strange way. It is to make poetry out of them, as in generating images through poetic diction, the real meaning of mounting the names 'in sequence on blank paper'.

But poetry does not mean simply making something formally beautiful out of the material to hand – though this happens too. What occurs is a deep acknowledgement of the power of nature, the moulding, destroying, bending and beating forces of nature. Anyone who has seen a 3-D model of the extraordinary cholinesterase molecule, its twists and turns, its hidden core and intricate links and chains, just has to agree – that it's like a poem, and it can create both fear and admiration in the face of its astonishing complexity. Just as 'Vocabulary' does, in its compacted history of the matching of the images and names of the dangerous flora and fauna living deep within all human minds, all human bodies.

Cards on the Table

James Wood, *The Irresponsible Self*
Pimlico
ISBN 1844130975

Gabriella Gruder-Poni

James Wood is that rare critic whom one may read with pleasure and profit even if one has not read the novel he's reviewing – indeed, whether or not one has any intention of reading it: his essays on mediocre works are as valuable as those on masterpieces. In this his second collection of essays, Wood traces the comedy of forgiveness from Shakespeare, whom he considers the essential progenitor of the English novel, to contemporary writers. The collection, roughly speaking, has a tripartite structure: it starts with Shakespeare and that other progenitor, Cervantes, and proceeds with essays on nineteenth- and early-twentieth-century European authors. The second half of the collection is devoted to fiction in English, but it does not proceed chronologically: essays on four authors who first made their mark over half a century ago – Saul Bellow, V.S. Naipaul, V.S. Pritchett, and Henry Green – come after essays on Zadie Smith, Salman Rushdie, Tom Wolfe, Jonathan Franzen, and Monica Ali. One surmises that Wood has buried his most topical, even incendiary, writings in the middle of the collection because his aim is not only to prod his contemporaries in what he considers to be the right direction and, occasionally, to point out that the emperor has no clothes, but also to draw our attention to some unjustly neglected authors: Saltykov-Shchedrin, Giovanni Verga, J.F. Powers, Henry Green. This neat balance – the humbling of the great coupled with the exaltation of the meek – is not the least of the many pleasures offered by *The Irresponsible Self.*

Perhaps Wood's chief virtue is the ability to explain, in detail, how and why a certain effect works. This is much harder to do than it sounds, and Wood gives a demonstration of his talent in the very first pages of the book when he explicates a joke. Comedy, as Wood notes, 'is often awarded the prize of ineffability,' but Wood amply proves that a joke can indeed be respectfully unfolded. It's a charmingly roundabout way into his topic, which is the difference between two kinds of comedy:

the comedy of correction ('laughing at,' or satire), and the comedy of forgiveness ('laughing with,' or tragicomedy), which Wood considers characteristic of the novel. Wood's next close reading is a concise and very astute examination of the humour in Erasmus's *In Praise of Folly*, a work that hovers between correction and forgiveness, and almost breaks apart under the strain of combining two incompatible modes. Like the rest of the book, this essay is fascinating, thought-provoking, and sometimes just plain provoking. As in his first collection, Wood rather stacks the deck against religion when he calls the comedy of correction ('the victory of knowing over the haze of unreliability') 'religious' comedy, and the far more sophisticated and humane comedy of forgiveness 'secular' comedy. Are religion and forgiveness, religion and unknowing really so antithetical? But whether or not one agrees with Wood's anti-theology his argument about the two kinds of comedy – whatever one calls them – is utterly convincing.

A short review can't really do justice to the scope and variety of this collection. It seems reasonable, therefore, to focus on the most topical of the essays, the ones on contemporary novelists. There are certain lines of continuity between *The Irresponsible Self* and Wood's first collection of essays, *The Broken Estate*: the freedom of characters (from an authorial agenda) is still dear to Wood: he writes of the 'unhostaged' Chekhov. And he takes his criticisms of Pynchon and DeLillo in *The Broken Estate* one step further in a comprehensive attack on 'hysterical realism.' Wood uses this term for a rather heterogeneous group of contemporary authors who, he believes, share the same besetting sins: fast and glib narration, a love of coincidence for its own sake and of random facts. In the collection's first essay on contemporary novelists Wood writes that the hysterical realists – a group that includes Rushdie, David Foster Wallace, and Zadie Smith, in addition to Pynchon and DeLillo – do not think that 'language and the representation of consciousness are the novelist's quarries anymore.' This much seems uncontroversial: Wood quotes Zadie Smith as saying that it is not the writer's job 'to tell us how somebody felt about something, it's to tell us how the world works.' For Wood this amounts to a cover-up, because hysterical realist novels seem 'evasive of reality while borrowing from realism itself.' The novels Wood criticizes purport to tell us about the world – politics, economics, the media, cutting-edge science – but their charm, their claim to novelty for many readers lies in their defiance of plausibility. A talking dog would be perfectly at home in a beast fable, and characters with significant birthmarks can be found by the score in children's books and fairytales; but to encounter these and similar freaks in a novel with all the trappings of realism is to feel put upon as a reader, as one would by a child who wants you to dry her tears and admire a neat trick all at once. These divided aims – cartoon, realism, satire, muck-raking – weaken one another, rob one another of legitimacy.

This is all quite complicated, but Wood untangles the issues – characters, cartoon, coincidences, the role of headline news in literature – with wit, eloquence, and lucidity. The attack on hysterical realism is really the first half of a surprisingly generous review of Zadie Smith's *White Teeth*, in which Wood praises precisely those moments when Smith allows her characters to be more than caricatures at the mercy of coincidences – presumably the moments which (to judge from Smith's public statements) she considers least noteworthy. It's a case of a critic trying to save a writer from her worst instincts: Wood considers Smith one of the most talented of the hysterical realists, and the article is as much an appeal to her as it is an attack on her colleagues.

Wood reserves his warmest praise for Jonathan Franzen and Monica Ali among contemporary novelists. Both *The Corrections* and *Brick Lane* build credit with their readers through the patient accumulation of 'quiddities,' to use Wood's word – psychological detail and moments of tragicomedy – so that when the time comes one willingly goes along with the characters' claims on one's sympathy. There is ample scope for comparison with Smith: *Brick Lane*, like *White Teeth*, is set in London's immigrant community; unlike Smith, Franzen believes that 'The writer of average talent who wants to report on, say, the plight of illegal aliens would be foolish to choose the novel as a vehicle.' Franzen has written extensively on his vision for the novel, and Wood's essay on Franzen is in part a response to 'Why Bother?', an essay published in *Harper's*, in which Franzen disavows the social novel and its fixation on topicality, and embraces a kind of timeless 'tragic realism.' Wood agrees with Franzen's conclusion, but finds his arguments weak. It's true that Franzen tacks back and forth between sociology, autobiography and criticism, and his voice is so charming it escapes one's notice that he often doesn't chase down an idea, but lets it scurry away when something else catches his eye – or when it would lead him to a conclusion that offends his anti-elitist instincts. Wood would like Franzen to give an assertive argument grounded in aesthetics, and Wood obligingly does this in his own essay. Reading the essays side by side one feels grateful towards Wood, but one wouldn't want Franzen to be *much* more coherent than he is, for his leaps of logic are true to the workings of the mind.

Most of Wood's insights are reached through close readings; so it seems fair to put the critic's prose under the microscope. And Wood is an accomplished stylist; his sentences are lean and nimble, and he has a direct, clear-eyed manner that makes the reader trust him. Though he doesn't offer up his personality as Franzen does, he lets us see his mind at work. He is often calm and witty; when he is impassioned or outraged he never lapses into pomposity. Some of his word choices are inspired: in Joseph Roth's *The Radetzky March* 'Lieutenant Trotta comes to represent an entire generation of enfeebled young men, living off the recessive heroism of an earlier imperial age.' 'Recessive' chimes with 'generation,' and implies that this inherited characteristic, heroism, shows up randomly in a very small minority of descendants. But the word also brings to mind its cousin, 'receding,' as if ranks of charging cavalry were being sucked into the distance. It's a very fine effect, a note that sets off echoes in two keys. Or of the praise that has greeted 'hysterical realist' novels, Wood writes: 'Bright lights are taken as evidence of habitation' – a metaphor that perfectly encapsulates the noise and glitter of these works, and the reader's disappointment upon discovering the emptiness behind the busy plots and the chattering narration. Other idiosyncratic word choices are less successful, as when Wood writes that 'English modernism can be measured in units of exhaustion.' How can modernism be measured? What's a unit of exhaustion? Wood is aiming for a marriage of hard and soft, accurate and elusive, a prose that knows emotion and feels thought, but he doesn't always pull it off. This is his only consistent failing, and it is far outweighed by his successes.

In his first collection, *The Broken Estate*, Wood explained his title in the epilogue, which seemed somehow to close down possibilities. ('Is that what all the essays were about?' one wondered at the end.) In *The Irresponsible Self* there is no epilogue; all the tying-together is done in the introduction – as if Wood had laid his cards on the table at the beginning of the game. The reader's sense of freedom is somewhat surprising, given that, as Wood tells us on the very first page, this collection, unlike his first, was conceived as a whole. He writes in the introduction, 'I wish to avoid over-assertion.' He does nevertheless over-assert. But whether or not one agrees with him, one has always a feeling that he would listen to one's objections; there was never the temptation to throw the book across the room; on the contrary, it is a pleasure to follow Wood's train of thought, and, in an argumentative mood, one could even welcome such intelligent provocations. Over-assertion, it seems, is a necessary effect of strong convictions.

Taste the Miles

William Fiennes, *The Snow Geese*
London: Picador, 2003

Matt Thomas

Natural history books are suddenly an endangered species. Which one is worth saving?

There are a few that spring to mind. *The Collins Bird Guide*, for example, is as essential as binoculars to the twitchers of Fair Isle in helping them search for a confused Pechora Pipit that has strayed across the North Sea. Similarly, Nick Baker's *New Amateur Naturalist* is excellent for anyone who would rather get more 'hands on' with the natural world as it includes many interesting ideas and projects. Oliver Rackham's *Illustrated History of the Countryside* is a superb book to dip into for fascinating facts about the British landscape.

But I am not a twitcher, I have no desire to fill my fridge with owl pellets and my interest in the origins of dry stone-walling are limited.

The books I have listed above, though, are very good. In fact, they are great for those who have a keen interest in the subject of natural history and wish to develop it further.

However, what about somebody who has seen Bill Oddie's *Springwatch* or the *Big Cat Diaries* and knows little of our environment, and wants to get started but is daunted by the complexity of ecology and wildlife? Also, it can be intimidating getting into wildlife watching as, more than with some other hobbies, experts tend to look down their binoculars at the beginner who is more impressed by a Goldfinch (common and colourful) than a Paddyfield Warbler (rare vagrant, but a little drab). I find this 'my optics are bigger than yours' attitude strange and unhelpful: surely those who know and appreciate the natural world should want to help those wishing to get back to nature? (Especially at a point when wildlife is facing a tough time due to global climate change.)

I want a book that will explain some of the wonders of the natural world, but not demystify them like a magician revealing the secrets of his show.

The book I would nominate for the last place on the ark can be called natural history reportage, a travel journal or simply a story. *The Snow Geese* by William Fiennes is beautifully written, informative and inspirational. Hopefully after reading it you will care if your local marsh is drained for that by-pass, or decide to join the RSPB.

The book starts with Fiennes ill in bed, and here he remains for some time. While out of action he reads about, and is amazed by, the migration of Snow Geese from the Gulf of Mexico, where they spend the winter, to the arctic tundras of Canada, where they breed. He decides that once fit he will shadow the birds on their mammoth journey. The book charts these twin expeditions.

On his travels he discovers the reasons why the birds take these amazing journeys twice a year, and explains how we found this out. He unravels the theories of displacement experiments and celestial navigation without sounding like a lecturer and remaining very readable.

Read this and you will be amazed by the feats of the geese and other migratory birds (e.g. the *non-stop* journeys of many tiny warblers from sub-Sarharan Africa to Northern Europe). Importantly, even though you have discovered the nuts and bolts behind the phenomenon of migration, none of the joy of seeing your summer's first swallow arriving from Africa is dampened. (If you become truly inspired there is an extensive bibliography that lists some excellent migration texts.)

His descriptions of the birds and their habitats are stunning and evocative. I am familiar with many of the species and ecosystems that Fiennes describes and they felt real to me and triggered personal memories of trips out into the wilds. His writing helped me to describe to others things I have seen but could not articulate:

> At Sand Lake Snow Geese had gathered on the ice in a great assembly.
>
> Two hundred thousand geese. More even. Two hundred and fifty thousand.
>
> We stood at the edge of the lake. Small groups of Canada Geese kept to the gold fringe of cattail and phrags. The ice was covered with snow geese: a thick sown crop of white necks, right across the lake. Goose calls resounded in the ice, as if the hollow, metallic din were trapped inside it. Sorties of geese took flight from the assembly; squads returned from nearby fields, coasting down on bowed wings and settling in the midst of

> the gaggle. Suddenly, the flock took wing, an audience breaking into applause. It was as if the ice itself had exploded [...] the flock seethed, rolling back and forth on itself, its shadow roiling like a turbulence on the ice below. (Fiennes, *The Snow Geese*, p. 109)

On his journey with the birds Fiennes meets many characters and has several adventures, creating a great travel story. His book is worth reading for this alone. However, you never forget that the stars of the book are the birds and their homes and that this is, for them, a matter of survival, not merely a story. You, as well as Fiennes, become involved with the birds' trials and tribulations, and end up willing them north to breed. His attachment to the birds is moving. At one point he is forced, reluctantly, to eat one of his quarry on the arctic wastes, and this is very poignant.

> We ate, sitting on the snow, leaning back against the shack [...] it had never occurred to me that I would have to eat a snow goose. I was attached to these birds. I couldn't help thinking of them as my companions. [...] The meat was rich: you could taste the miles in it. The morsels sat in my stomach like pebbles. We ate in silence, snug in our parkas, snow geese inside and out. (p. 233)

If this book moves you to get out and about, to just look at the natural world, then you will learn more than if you scour every last page of ten field guides, and that is why it is so good.

Environmental and conservation issues are often pushed to one side, so if there were just one space left on the shelf for a natural history book then I would choose *The Snow Geese*.

However, if I was stranded on a desert island and could only have one book I would choose the *Field Guide to Obscure Desert Island Birds* by A. Twitcher, obviously.

Over the land freckled with snow half-thawed
The speculating rooks at their nests cawed
And saw from elm-tops, delicate as flower of grass,
What we below could not see, Winter pass.
(Edward Thomas, 'Thaw')

Revelations of Uncertainty

Andrea Levy, *Small Island*
Hodder Headline
ISBN 075530750X

Linda Taylor

This book was winner of both the Whitbread Book of the Year and the 2004 Orange Prize, and it is a genuinely good read. It tells the story of the Jamaicans who chose to fight for their 'mother country' in the Second World War, and of the great change in their reception when they returned to settle in Britain after the war. *Small Island* deals with this racism and with the conflict of cultures but it is not a preaching book – there is a real warmth and humour underlying the recounting of the tale.

The story centres on a white British married couple, Queenie and Bernard, and a black Jamaican married couple, Hortense and Gilbert. Levy uses the device of allowing the four central characters to narrate the story, often relaying the same incident from their very different perspectives. The effect is not so much to fragment the tale as to make real the human complexity. There is an intimacy in the narratives as the characters reveal not only their views of the events around them but also their internal selves. This shows us their vulnerability and fragility – not always evident to the other characters – and we warm to them. This is particularly true of the proud and prickly Hortense and the less than charismatic character of Bernard. Our first introduction to Bernard, for example, is through the narration of his wife Queenie. He appears as a rather dull and unemotional bank clerk, but, when Bernard speaks himself, we see his emotional dependence on his wife and his feeling of inadequacy in relation to her, and because of this we feel sympathy for him. When he joins the RAF, for instance, and is unable to fly due to his poor eyesight, he says: 'She would have liked to live with a hero. I knew that much for a fact.' In a very touching scene near the end of the book he tells us, 'I knew it: she was always too good for me.'

The issues around race are complex and are really about internal and external identity. Levy contrasts the experiences of the Jamaican men fighting as part of the British army and that of the black

American soldiers. The Jamaican soldiers are baffled by the racism they encounter and their expected role as the underclass or second-class citizens, and they don't understand the black American soldiers' acceptance of the role. There is also the great contrast between the British view of the Jamaican men in uniform and the subsequent view of Gilbert as 'threatening' when he returns as a civilian after the war. There is a moving passage in which Gilbert relates a string of incidents of racist behaviour towards other Jamaicans he knows. He feels the coldness both of the harsh British weather and also of the British people, and he longs for the physical and emotional warmth of home. It's particularly moving because Gilbert is normally so buoyant. Typically, it is a small act of human kindness which saves Gilbert from his depression, as a stranger offers him a sweet to cheer and warm him. He tells us, 'it was a salvation to me – not for the sugar but the act of kindness. The human tenderness with which it was given to me.'

Another thread in the book is the strong paralleling of the two women. Both have opted to marry to escape from their former lives: for Queenie, marriage allows her escape from the farm that is so unsuited to her temperament, and for Hortense it allows the longed-for adventure of coming to England. Neither felt their dream could be achieved without a husband, but for both marriage in turn brings its problems. There are many moments of comedy between the two women as Queenie's well-meaning and often patronising attempts to befriend Hortense inflame the haughty Jamaican woman, who considers herself to be superior in every way. It is often Hortense who tells us of their conversations, and her affronted attitude superbly enforces the comic effect. Early in their relationship, Queenie assures Hortense 'You'll soon get used to our language.' Hortense responds, 'I told this Englishwoman I can speak the English language very well thank you.' But Queenie completely misses the fact that she has offended Hortense and continues: 'No need to thank me… I'm sure there's a lot I could teach you, if you wanted.' Hortense is horrified by Queenie not only making herself at home but also taking the liberty of inviting Hortense to sit with her in Hortense's own home. Hortense concludes that in fact it is Queenie who could learn from her: 'I could surely teach this woman something… Manners!' But in contrast to what she has just said with such pride and conviction, Hortense then shows her vulnerability: 'But then I questioned. Maybe this is how the English do things when in England? So I sat.' It is these small revelations of uncertainty which make us warm to the characters.

Hortense later describes Queenie's first shopping trip with her. Queenie reassures her, 'It's all right. I don't mind being seen in the street with you. You'll find I'm not like most. It doesn't worry me to be seen out with darkies.' Hortense is mystified: 'Now why should this woman worry to be seen in the street with me? After all, I was a teacher and she was only a woman whose living was obtained from the letting of rooms.' It is interesting to see that Hortense herself has a great deal of prejudice, but in her case it is in relation to class and education. She sees the less educated Queenie as inferior, although because of her revealed vulnerability we can see that this is in part a defence mechanism for Hortense. Her often-repeated assertions of her superiority are, we feel, as much to convince herself as to convince the reader. Despite their differences, however, the two women do finally, in a rather unexpected way, achieve a level of trust and understanding.

The detailed observation of the couples' relationships is a real strength of the book – the poignant moments of missed opportunities for understanding and rapprochement, and other moments when brief contact is made. Tiny gestures are given significance in their bleak context. A good example of this is when Hortense, having experienced a bitter disappointment, says rather desperately to Gilbert, 'I dreamed of coming to London.' His response to Hortense, as often, is flippant and inappropriate: 'Well there you see, not many people have a dream come true.' However, for once the isolated and miserable Hortense accepts his good intentions, as Gilbert tells us: 'It was a timid hand I stretched across the table to place over hers. I waited for her to slap it away. But she did not.' This small lack of rejection achieves a great significance in his eyes.

There are many examples of misunderstandings between the other couple, the passionate Queenie and the unemotional Bernard. A good example is their differing views of the scene when Bernard leaves to go to war. Queenie tells us, 'I wanted to hug him, whisper into his ear... But he stiffened like a plank of best mahogany, then bent to kiss my cheek.' As she watches him leave she says, 'The pity of it was he wouldn't have known that I was watching him through the window, let alone that I was worrying. And when he was finally out of view, the road screamed with emptiness.' She is correct: Bernard is unaware of her concern and tells us of the same occasion, 'She'd shut the front door behind me before I'd got down to the last step'. There is a wistfulness in both accounts which is very moving.

It is a touchingly human story. Initially, we would naturally think that the 'Small Island' of the title was Jamaica. But in many ways those from the small island of Jamaica are depicted as having a much broader view of life than the small-minded white British people. We are left wondering about the island of the title. It seems to me it could refer as easily to Jamaica, to Britain, to those with bigoted views, or indeed to each of the strangely isolated characters speaking to us; they are all, in a sense, small islands.

Trying to Tuck My Continent in Behind Me

Karen Press, *The Canary's Songbook*
Carcanet, 2005
ISBN 1 85754 7632

Mary Weston

Karen Press is a South African poet. She writes about trauma (personal and public), about ancestors and the past, and about corruption. Knowing all this it can take a certain amount of self-discipline to approach her poems, as it would to start reading a long and highly informative article about one of her continent's tragedies – AIDS or famine or genocide. But you force yourself, and it's not that bad. Press has a dry, occasionally droll tone of voice and a sharp eye for the little hypocrisies of the dinner party:

> He can't explain, so he just says
> 'I'm writing about corruption'
> and everyone at the table goes 'ah'.
> They're glad, as if now that a poet is taking it on
> something might happen

or the international conference:

> You wish you could have a miracle like ours,
> Sort of atom bomb of festivity to clear the past out of
> the way.

But when she tackles bigger, worse subjects for which this dry humour is inappropriate, her indignation and her rhythms can sound flat-footed:

> The cheapness of the songs they teach this child
> is where it starts. They make her clap her hands,
> they make her sing 'My bodee is my bodee',
> they make her smile at the TV cameras like a rescued
> seal.

> The little girl is sewn onto the letterheads and T-shirts
> of the Ministry of Health, the Ministry of Welfare and
> the Ministry of Education.
> Tonight her father and her uncle and her teacher will rip
> her off the T-shirts
> push her head into the cushion and rape her.

I find her more believable when she writes most inwardly of trauma:

> Is there a moment
> when you feel better,
> cured?
>
> Glass glued together
> still edges carefully
> along its shatter lines…
>
> Love and loneliness and longing
> sparkle like bad clusters
> inside the alienated lightness of you.
>
> What was there before?
> It's gone.
> Try not to tear your shadow open, looking for it.

And because of course the 'atom bomb' of South African liberation didn't really destroy the past, Press is particularly rewarding when looking at history, at the way it reaches into us now – and best when she images this through the concept of one's ancestors:

> At night the ancestors pay their way
> by sending me dreams.
> I wake up having been in so many former living rooms
>
> I have no idea how to redecorate my house
> or what to do with the garden,
> and several letters of apology seem necessary.

'Are séances held by the dead to call up the living?' she asks elsewhere. When she feels free to be light, her writing comes in from surprising and illuminating angles. The poem I liked best in this collection is a piece about the Chinese T'ang dynasty poet Li Po. I love the way that Press edges suggestively around what makes the author of 'The Drunkard in Spring' different from every other piss artist:

the ones that phone you late at night,
who send their works unfinished, who make you drive
for hours –

without trying to define it or spell it out. I love it most of all for its title, 'He is often mentioned in books.'

A Handful of Titles

Tom Turner, *Garden History: Philosophy and Design 2000BC – 2000AD*
Spar Press, 2005

Ede Harter

This handsomely produced book seeks to show how garden design finds its place within, inevitably, rather broadly sketched histories of society and thought. It is lavishly illustrated though the photographs are small. Most usefully, it offers a great number of plans of historic gardens. For designers it will be a stimulus to reflection and a source of ideas. With a comparable geographical breadth Roger Phillips and Nicky Foy, *A Photographic Garden History* (Macmillan, 1995) would provide a useful supplement.

The subject is now so specialised that I would mention a few mainly out-of-print books, more general in scope. On the narratives of specific plants, Alice Coats, *Flowers and their Histories* (1956) and *Garden Shrubs and their Histories* (1963), warms the heart and informs the mind. Miles Hadfield, *A History of British Gardening* (1969) offers the kind of absorbing detail you would expect of a man who was himself a practical gardener. Anthony Huxley's *Illustrated History of Gardening* (1983) discusses the actual processes and tools of cultivation. But one of the best histories ever written was one of the first, Alicia Amherst, *A History of Gardening in England* (1895), especially for its references to early sources – eight of its thirteen chapters take the reader only to the close of the sixteenth century – and its chronology of garden books down to 1837.

> The biographer warned himself: It's one thing for a man not to know, not to have learned; it's another not to be able to live by what one does know.
>
> (Bernard Malamud, from *Dubin's Lives*)

Henry David Thoreau: The True Harvest

Ann Stapleton

> Perhaps the facts most astounding and most real are never communicated by man to man. The true harvest of my daily life is somewhat as intangible and indescribable as the tints of morning or evening. It is a little star-dust caught, a segment of the rainbow which I have clutched.
>
> Henry David Thoreau

Just a week shy of twenty-nine when he began his experiment at Walden Pond (1845–1847), Henry David Thoreau was old enough to have suffered significant losses. In 1840, his marriage proposal to Ellen Sewall, to whom his brother John had already proposed, was rejected. (To the everlasting benefit of American literature, one might suppose, Sewall's father prevailed upon her to have nothing to do with those wild, freethinking Thoreau boys.) And in 1842, John, the dear companion of Henry's youth, contracted tetanus from a rusty razor cut and died in his brother's arms. Afterward Thoreau experienced weeks of a psychosomatic paralysis that mimicked the one John had endured, and then underwent a period of severe depression. 'The shock, the loss, and the sight of his brother's terrible suffering at the end, for a time overthrew Henry so utterly that a friend told me he sat still in the house, could do nothing, and his sisters led him out passive to try to help him,' wrote Ralph Waldo Emerson's son Edward. 'Near the same time died suddenly a beautiful child [the Emersons' Waldo, five years old], with whom he had played and talked almost daily.'

All of which is not to say that Thoreau's time in the woods signified a retreat from human feeling or a descent into extended mourning (he made it quite clear on the title page that *Walden* was not to be 'an ode to dejection'), but is simply to note that he had, however reluctantly, already been released from some of his strongest bonds of affection. Unacceptable to Ellen, unnecessary to John, and temperamentally unsuited to the conciliations of village life, with its inhabitants sometimes more alien to him than 'Sandwich Islanders,' he was free (enough) to begin the experiment of a lifetime: 'I went to the woods because I wished to live deliberately, to front only the essential facts of life, and see if I could not learn what it had to teach, and not, when I came to die, discover that I had not lived.'

Thoreau's Concord, Massachusetts, was a center of intellectual fervency in his day, the place where a new American literature was (quite deliberately) being founded, and home to the leading lights of Transcendentalism, with its emphasis on nature, social reform, and self-fulfillment. In addition to Ralph Waldo Emerson, the movement's mainstay (and owner of the land on Walden Pond where Thoreau built his cabin), Henry was in contact with Nathaniel Hawthorne (and he with Herman Melville); A. Bronson Alcott (who advocated such radical educational reforms as allowing students to speak and ask questions in class and doing away with corporal punishment) and his daughter, Louisa May Alcott (who may have proposed marriage to Henry); Walt Whitman (whom Thoreau described as 'A remarkably strong though coarse nature, of a sweet disposition, and much prized by his friends'); and the brilliant early feminist (Sarah) Margaret Fuller (whose body and manuscripts Thoreau was sent to retrieve, though he was unable to, when she and her husband and child perished in a shipwreck). A little further away from Concord, in Amherst, influenced by the writings of the Transcendentalists and admiring enough of Thoreau to pen a poem about the 'fighting for his Life' he was doing 'In that Campaign inscrutable / Of the Interior' in which she, too, had enlisted, Emily Dickinson, relieved by eccentricity of the curse of self-prohibition and following the prescriptions of her genius, was writing her letter to the world – a dubious enterprise of which the Transcendentalists would have approved heartily.

'I am naturally no hermit,' Thoreau expressly pointed out, and though he took pleasure in (and was highly productive as a result of) his solitary state, even during his days at Walden Pond he was strongly connected to others. He was an intimate of the Emersons, living with the family for two years as their handyman and gardener, and later staying with Lydia and the children for ten months while Emerson lectured abroad. (Thoreau's letters express a deep love for Lydia, but there is no evidence to suggest that the relationship was other than platonic.) He was an impressive, oracular presence even in his circle of eminences ('Such dangerous frankness was in his dealing that his admirers called him "that terrible Thoreau," as if he spoke when silent, and was still present when he had departed,' wrote Emerson). And he was an involved and caring son and brother who was wonderful with children, as described here by Edward Emerson, his unofficial little brother:

> This youthful, cheery figure was a familiar one in our house, and when he, like the 'Pied Piper of Hamelin,' sounded his note in the hall, the children must needs come and hug his knees, and he struggled with them, nothing loath, to the fireplace, sat down and told stories, sometimes of the strange adventures of his childhood, or more often of squirrels, muskrats, hawks, he had seen that day, the Monitor-and-Merrimac duel of mud-turtles in the river, or the great Homeric battle of the red and black ants. Then he would make our pencils and knives disappear, and redeem them presently from our ears and noses; and last, would bring down the heavy copper warming-pan from the oblivion of the garret and unweariedly shake it over the blaze till reverberations arose within, and then opening it, let a white-blossoming explosion of popcorn fall over the little people on the rug.

Thoreau, who built his cabin with his own hands, understood early on that, as a house comes into being board by board, so a man is built by the books he reads, each period a nail, each strip of white between the lines a chinking of silence:

> There are probably words addressed to our condition exactly, which, if we could really hear and understand, would be more salutary than the morning or the spring to our lives, and possibly put a new aspect on the face of things for us. How many a man has dated a new era in his life from the reading of a book! The book exists for us, perchance, which will explain our miracles and reveal new ones. The at present unutterable things we may find somewhere uttered.

Thoreau considered the written word to be his (and everyone else's) absolute birthright. Edward Emerson writes that Thoreau at Harvard 'saw that the curriculum was narrow, and to make the sacrifice worth while he must not stick too closely to it,' and that 'even although the loss of marks involved nearly cost the important relief of a scholarship and brought some disapproval of his teachers, he deliberately devoted much of his time to the College library.' And Ralph Waldo Emerson, in his eulogy for Thoreau, notes that when Henry, graduated from Harvard and no longer legally able to borrow books, was denied in the attempt, he reacted with the ferocity of a trapped wild creature, using his version of claws and teeth (his words!) to fight for what to him was essential to his survival, the words of others:

> Mr. Thoreau explained to the President… that the library was useless, yes, and President and College useless, on the terms of his rules, – that the one benefit he owed to the College was its library, – that, at this moment, not only his want of books was imperative, but he wanted a large number of books, and assured him that he, Thoreau, and not the librarian, was the proper custodian of these. In short, the President found the petitioner so formidable, and the rules getting to look so ridiculous, that he ended by giving him a privilege which in his hands proved unlimited thereafter.

Thoreau believed that 'Books must be read as deliberately and reservedly as they [are] written.' He advocated reading always above ourselves, not what we already know, but those books 'we have to stand on tip-toe to read and devote our most alert and wakeful hours to.' Patrician in his reading tastes, preferring Homer and Dante and Shakespeare and the ancient classics, he was nevertheless fiercely egalitarian in insisting that the writer speaks 'to all in any age who can understand him.' He lectured at the Concord Lyceum and was an early proponent of continuing education: 'It is time that we had uncommon schools, that we did not leave off our education when we begin to be men and women. It is time that villages were universities, and their elder inhabitants the fellows of universities, with leisure […] to pursue liberal studies the rest of their lives.' And he believed communities should be willing to pay for the privilege: 'If it is necessary, omit one bridge over the river, go round a little there, and throw one arch at least over the darker gulf of ignorance which surrounds us.'

Yet the philosopher-poet of Walden Pond who lived so happily in his head could also be practical when necessary. He could easily repair all manner of things, and was a skilled and sought-after surveyor. In order to increase his family's financial security, he made ingenious, state of the art improvements to their pencil-making business, adding clay to the graphite and creating a machine that would insert the lead without causing the wood to split. He even invented the grading system that gives us our #2 pencils.

He also possessed a keen, understated sense of humor not always apparent to his neighbors. When *A Week on the Concord and Merrimack Rivers*, the record of the last trip he took with John, failed to sell, he was philosophical: 'I have now a library of nearly nine hundred volumes, over seven hundred of which I wrote myself.'

And when he was dying of tuberculosis, his Calvinist aunt asked, 'Henry, have you made your peace with God?' His answer: 'I was not aware we had ever quarreled.'

Thoreau carried on a spirited and lifelong argument with the status quo: the naturalist William Burroughs said of him that 'In the great army of Mammon, the great army of the fashionable, the complacent and church-going, Thoreau was a skulker, even a deserter, if you please – yea, a traitor fighting on the other side.' In 1846 he was jailed for a night for refusing, in protest against slavery and the Mexican War, to pay his poll tax. His essay 'Civil Disobedience' ('Let your life be a counter friction to stop the machine') powerfully influenced both Mahatma Gandhi and Martin Luther King.

As is characteristic of a great debater, he did not readily cede points to the institutions and personalities he perceived as his opponents. But rather than being a detriment to his writing, the sureties of one-sidedness are actually the basis of its strength and humanity. Opposites and absolutes were Thoreau's consuming interest and his area of expertise, and he spoke eloquently and compellingly on behalf of them: of poverty ('Superfluous wealth can buy superfluities only. Money is not required to buy one necessary of the soul') and solitude ('I have a great deal of company in my house; especially in the morning, when nobody calls'); of the misfit ('If a man does not keep pace with his companions, perhaps it is because he hears a different drummer. Let him step to the music which he hears, however measured or far away') and the animal ('No humane being, past the thoughtless age of boyhood, will wantonly murder any creature which holds its life by the same tenure that he does. The hare in its extremity cries like a child'); and even, as 'attorney of the indigenous plants,' as Emerson described him, for mute nature ('We need the tonic of wildness [...] We need to witness our own limits transgressed, and some life pasturing freely where we never wander').

Though Thoreau was perhaps America's most eloquent explicator of solitude's compensations, an alert reader will find the tracks of his loneliness there along the pond's edge, though he brushed them over for our benefit. Referring to a custom from the *Vishnu Purana*, a Hindu religious text, in which 'The house-holder is to remain at eventide in his courtyard as long as it takes to milk a cow, or longer if he pleases, to await the arrival of a guest,' Thoreau writes, 'There too, as everywhere, I sometimes expected the Visitor who never comes [...] I often performed this duty of hospitality, waited long enough to milk a whole herd of cows, but did not see the man approaching from the town.' In a similar rare moment, Thoreau acknowledges in this mysterious passage of pure longing all things loved and lost and never to be found again:

> I long ago lost a hound, a bay horse, and a turtle dove, and am still on their trail. Many are the travelers I have spoken concerning them, describing their tracks and what calls they answered to. I have met one or two who had heard the hound, and the tramp of the horse, and even seen the dove disappear behind a cloud, and they seemed as anxious to recover them as if they had lost them themselves.

Thoreau and his family were active in the Underground Railroad. In addition to lecturing against slavery, speaking out on behalf of the radical abolitionist John Brown, with whom he once had lunch, and even helping one of Brown's men to escape to Canada, Thoreau himself hid fugitive slaves and helped them on to safety, as in Edward Emerson's relation of a story told by Moncure D. Conway, a 'brave young Virginian preacher' who lived near the Thoreaus 'when a hunted slave came to the village by night to the home of that family':

> When I went [there] next morning, I found them all in a state of excitement by reason of the arrival of a fugitive negro from the South, who had come fainting to their door about daybreak and thrown himself upon their mercy [...] I sat and watched the singularly tender and lowly devotion of the scholar to the slave. He must be fed, his swollen feet bathed, and he must think of nothing but rest: again and again this coolest and calmest of men drew near to the trembling negro, and soothed him and bade him feel at home, and have no fear that any power should again wrong him. Thoreau could not walk with me that day, as had been agreed, but must mount guard over the fugitive, for slave-hunters were not extinct in those days, and so I went away, after a while, much impressed by many little traits that I had seen as they appeared in this emergency.

Thoreau tenderly nursed through their dying days not only his brother John, but also his father, and he was on fond terms with all the natural world. He played water tag with a loon, shared his table with a mouse ('when at last I held still a piece of cheese between my thumb and finger, it came and nibbled it, sitting in my hand'), and let the birds flit through his cabin. He 'grieved' for fallen trees and looked 'at his woodpile with a kind of affection.' Thoreau would have been a remarkable man had he never picked up a pen at all. But, of course, he did.

In a review of *Walden* written for *Westminster Review* in 1856, George Eliot, whose own life and thought persistently outpaced the village mentality in its slow progress along the beaten path, hails a fellow outlaw sensibility from the woods of the New World, praising Thoreau's 'energetic, yet calm spirit of innovation, that practical as well as theoretic independence of formulae, which is peculiar to some of the finer American minds.' In particular, she notes that his 'observations of natural phenomena are not only made by a keen eye, but have their interest enhanced by passing through the medium of a deep poetic sensibility.'

Given Eliot's uncommon gifts and the isolation she experienced as a woman in unorthodox relation to family and society, she might well have felt a kinship with this refined yet very free man, living remote from the daily ebb and flow, segregated from normalcy by the implacable authenticities of genius. Both worked on in the wilderness of the self with optimism and devotion, and, far from abandoning those who could not keep pace, were magnanimous enough in spirit to send back eloquent and encouraging dispatches to anyone willing to read and be changed. Writing of Thoreau's critics, Eliot would have understood only too well the tyranny of 'People – very wise in their own eyes – who would have every man's life ordered according to a particular pattern, and who are intolerant of every existence the utility of which is not palpable to them.'

In the brief space of a one-paragraph review, she puts her finger on perhaps the most essential aspect of Thoreau's considerable literary endowment: his 'deep poetic sensibility.' Though he wrote verse throughout his life ('Light-winged Smoke, Icarian bird, / Melting thy pinions in thy upward flight'), he was not a gifted poet. As Emerson put it, 'he no doubt wanted a lyric facility and technical skill'. But as Eliot was quick to notice, Thoreau's way of seeing, though informed by a naturalist's attentiveness, was essentially that of the poet (lyrical, metaphorical, in love with the particulars that lead us deeper into meaning). If he was a mere rhymester when he turned his attentions to versifying, he was, paradoxically, the truest poet when he turned to prose, as in this almost heroically compressed but electric description not only of a rainbow's discrete loveliness but the ecstatic quality of its penetration of his soul, and of beauty's power to transform or even unhinge the life open enough to receive it:

> Once it chanced that I stood in the very abutment of a rainbow's arch, which filled the lower stratum of the

> atmosphere, tinging the grass and leaves around, and dazzling me as if I looked through colored crystal. It was a lake of rainbow light, in which, for a short while, I lived like a dolphin. If it had lasted longer it might have tinged my employments and life.

Who has ever watched a dolphin, so at home in the water, without envying the sheer freedom and belonging of its movements and receiving from the oneness of animal and element an overpowering sense of the two-legged clumsiness, the partial commitment with which human beings embrace or flee their fates? Yet the experience also evokes an immediate, joyful entry into the greater miracle (however you describe it to yourself) that engenders it. And it is this stepping out of our awkwardness and into our joy, regardless of what occasions it, that the generous Thoreau – often at one remove from his fellow man, but at home on his own in that other, wilder kind of belonging – wants for us all.

Thoreau's work is a hymn to interconnectedness. Consider how the following passage begins in his detailed notation of the world before him, then spirals down deeper into economics and the human cost of the (to him) inexplicable bad bargains we humans make, penetrating finally to an utterly strange and disturbing bedrock image of the taming of the American West that suddenly pulls the pain of all human progress from the very grass beneath your feet:

> I went a-graping to the river meadows, and loaded myself with clusters more precious for their beauty and fragrance than for food. There, too, I admired, though I did not gather, the cranberries, small waxen gems, pendants of the meadow grass, pearly and red, which the farmer plucks with an ugly rake, leaving the smooth meadow in a snarl, heedlessly measuring them by the bushel and the dollar only, and sells the spoils of the meads to Boston and New York; destined to be jammed, to satisfy the tastes of lovers of Nature there. So butchers rake the tongues of bison out of the prairie grass, regardless of the torn and drooping plant.

The plant's fate symbolizes the soullessness of economic necessity, the decline of the indigenous way of life, the demise of the West and (worse yet, in Thoreau's mind) the loss of wildness itself, and yet his scrupulous descriptions of natural phenomena and his fearless exploration of the higher reaches of human thought are filtered always through one man's days, and thus create the possibility of connection to the struggles of every human life. He wrote that 'If you have built castles in the air, your work need not be lost; that is where they should be. Now put the foundations under them,' and in a true sense, this describes his contribution to Transcendentalism. That with a poet's impassioned perception he unites the purely natural and the purely philosophical and finds occasion for their expression in the personal is what accounts for his greatness. The bison tongues are not only the tongues of bison, or the symbolic discards of human progress. Be careful what you trade for in your own life, too, he warns. What you end up with will be only what you insist upon, and what you stand to lose is always far more than you could have imagined.

William Burroughs notes that 'Thoreau brings the stars as near as any writer I know of,' and he was always glad to share their light. 'The stars are the apexes of what wonderful triangles!' he writes in *Walden*, marveling at 'What distant and different beings in the various mansions of the universe are contemplating the same one at the same moment!' And this is perhaps the most useful metaphor for the relation of Thoreau to his reader: though apart in time, they yet remain connected by his words, each to the other, and both to the highest brightness discernible from earth. Look up!, he counsels. Among the stars, you will recognize your own true life. As he did with the strangers who were welcome to his unlocked cabin even when he was not at home, Thoreau, the 'hermit,' though dead now almost a century and a half, is still sharing Walden Pond, is still making new friends, as can be seen in these messages left for him on a website containing a photograph of his original gravestone, marked simply, as if there could be no other, HENRY:

> – Hey Henry, I saw you the other day. I sat beside you and arranged the flowers.
> – HOPE TO WALK WITH YOU IN WALDEN WOODS SOMEDAY R.I.P.
> – I sometimes 'step to a different drummer, the music which I hear'
> – Thank you for everything, Beloved Henry.
> – I HOPE YOU FOUND PEACE

Thoreau

From *Atlantic Monthly* vol. 10 (August 1862)

Ralph Waldo Emerson

Had his genius been only contemplative, he had been fitted to his life, but with his energy and practical ability he seemed born for great enterprise and for command; and I so much regret the loss of his rare powers of action, that I cannot help counting it a fault in him that he had no ambition. Wanting this, instead of engineering for all America, he was the captain of a huckleberry-party. Pounding beans is good to the end of pounding empires one of these days; but if, at the end of years, it is still only beans!

But these foibles, real or apparent, were fast vanishing in the incessant growth of a spirit so robust and wise, and which effaced its defeats with new triumphs. His study of Nature was a perpetual ornament to him, and inspired his friends with curiosity to see the world through his eyes, and to hear his adventures. They possessed every kind of interest.

He had many elegancies of his own, whilst he scoffed at conventional elegance. Thus, he could not bear to hear the sound of his own steps, the grit of gravel; and therefore never willingly walked in the road, but in the grass, on mountains and in woods. His senses were acute, and he remarked that by night every dwelling-house gives out bad air, like a slaughter-house. He liked the pure fragrance of melilot. He honoured certain plants with special regard, and, over all, the pond-lily, – then, the gentian, and the *Mikania scandens*, and 'life-everlasting,' and a bass-tree which he visited every year when it bloomed, in the middle of July. He thought the scent a more oracular inquisition than the sight, – more oracular and trustworthy. The scent, of course, reveals what is concealed from the other senses. By it he detected earthiness. He delighted in echoes, and said they were almost the only kind of kindred voices that he heard. He loved Nature so well, was so happy in her solitude, that he became very jealous of cities and the sad work which their refinements and artifices made with man and his dwelling. The axe was always destroying his forest. 'Thank God,' he said, 'they cannot cut down the clouds!' 'All kinds of figures are drawn on the blue ground with this fibrous white paint.' …

There is a flower known to botanists, one of the same genus with our summer plant called 'Life-Everlasting,' a *Gnaphalium* like that, which grows on the most inaccessible cliffs of the Tyrolese mountains, where the chamois dare hardly venture, and which the hunter, tempted by its beauty, and by his love (for it is immensely valued by the Swiss maidens), climbs the cliffs to gather, and is sometimes found dead at the foot, with the flower in his hand. It is called by the botanists *Gnaphalium leontopodium*, but by the Swiss *Edelweisse*, which signifies *Noble Purity*. Thoreau seemed to me living in the hope to gather this plant, which belonged to him of right. The scale on which his studies proceeded was so large as to require longevity. The country knows not yet, or in the least part, how great a son it has lost. It seems an injury that he should leave in the midst his broken task which none else can finish, a kind of indignity to so noble a soul that he should depart out of Nature before yet he has been really shown to his peers for what he is. But he, at least, is content. His soul was made for the noblest society; he had in a short life exhausted the capabilities of this world; wherever there is knowledge, wherever there is virtue, wherever there is beauty, he will find a home.

> He was alone in the cosmos and desperately needed anyone, even a friend.
>
> (Bernard Malamud, from *Dubin's Lives*)

Carson McCullers, *The Member of the Wedding*

Helen Tookey

The kitchen, they say, is the heart of a house. For novelists of America's Deep South, the kitchen is frequently the tiny but symbolically loaded space in which writers can explore the family secrets, intimate relationships and tangled power-lines at the heart of Southern lives, through the eyes of the two kinds of people who inhabit these kitchens: white children, and the black servants who care for them. We can think, for example, of the Compson children and Dilsey, Luster and T.T. in Faulkner's *The Sound and the Fury*; of Joel Knox and Zoo Fever in Truman Capote's *Other Voices, Other Rooms*; of Jem and Scout Finch and Calpurnia in *To Kill a Mockingbird*; more recently, of the Cleve children and Ida Rhew in Donna Tartt's *The Little Friend*. The reason, I think, why this configuration comes up so often is that it gives us such a powerfully slant perspective on the doings of those who are in charge in this society: the white adults. The children through whose bewildered eyes we see are outsiders by virtue of their youth; they are awaiting their turn to inherit social power (to varying degrees, of course, depending on their sex); meanwhile, they observe, but they do not understand. The black servants who care for them, on the other hand, are outsiders in quite a different way: they understand the world of white folk's power, but they will never inherit this power.

One of the most compelling novels of the South to use this setting is Carson McCullers' *The Member of the Wedding*, first published in 1946. McCullers' writing often focuses on misfits and outsiders: the deaf mute John Singer and the tomboy Mick in *The Heart is a Lonely Hunter*; lonely Miss Amelia and the hunchback Cousin Lymon in *The Ballad of the Sad Café*. But for me her most moving, and memorable, fictional character is twelve-year-old Frankie Addams, the protagonist of this short and strange book.

The book revolves around Frankie, her six-year-old cousin John Henry West, and the cook Berenice Sadie Brown; and, although we do follow Frankie around her small town and on the five-hour bus ride to the disastrous wedding in Winter Hill, the heart of the book is obsessively, claustrophobically – and movingly – fixed in the kitchen, where the three of them have spent most of the summer.

This is how the book begins:

> It happened that green and crazy summer when Frankie was twelve years old. This was the summer when for a long time she had not been a member. She belonged to no club and was a member of nothing in the world. Frankie had become an unjoined person who hung around in doorways, and she was afraid. In June the trees were bright dizzy green, but later the leaves darkened, and the town turned black and shrunken under the glare of the sun. At first Frankie walked around doing one thing and another. The sidewalks of the town were gray in the early morning and at night, but the noon sun put a glaze on them, so that the cement burned and glittered like glass. The sidewalks finally became too hot for Frankie's feet, and also she got herself in trouble. She was in so much secret trouble that she thought it was better to stay at home – and at home there was only Berenice Sadie Brown and John Henry West. The three of them sat at the kitchen table, saying the same things over and over, so that by August the words began to rhyme with each other and sound strange. The world seemed to die each afternoon and nothing moved any longer. At last the summer was like a green sick dream, or like a silent crazy jungle under glass. And then, on the last Friday of August, all this was changed: it was so sudden that Frankie puzzled the whole blank afternoon, and still she did not understand.

I have quoted this opening paragraph in its entirety to try to convey the unique quality of McCullers' prose – and to show how, on the first page of the book, she draws the reader so completely inside Frankie's world and the world of the book itself. McCullers writes with the same apparently simple rhythms as, say, Flannery O'Connor, seeming to echo the thought- and speech-rhythms of the South: 'The sidewalks finally became too hot for Frankie's feet, and also she got herself in trouble'. At the same time her phrasings are often strange and disconcerting, as seen in the very title of this book: how can one become a member of a wedding? What does it mean to say that 'Frankie had become an unjoined person... and she was afraid'? McCullers has the ability to depict a world that is at one and the same time utterly real, and entirely language-bound. We can see this perfectly in this first paragraph, with its description of a summer at once so hot that the pavements burn feet, and 'like a green, sick dream', a world that 'seem[s] to die each afternoon'. Reading this book is a kind of double reading: reading *through* the language to the reality of the world pictured, to Frankie and Berenice and John Henry and the tragedy that, in different ways, they each experience; and at the same time reading *within* the language, the almost tactile experience of moving amongst the words that McCullers puts together in such extraordinary ways.

The Member of the Wedding is a short book and can easily be read in one sitting. Yet it contains profound meditations on growing up, on fitting in (or not fitting in) to adult society with all its structures and frameworks; on identity, what it means to be the unique person that you inescapably are (as Berenice puts it, 'We all of us somehow caught. We born this way or that way and we don't know why'); on time, and love, and death. The book tells the story of Frankie, the 'unjoined person', who falls in love with the idea of her brother's impending wedding and with the idea of *belonging*, by means of this wedding, not so much to the couple themselves, Jarvis and Janice, as to the structures they represent (in Berenice's words, 'they looked natural... They make a nice white couple'). Frankie is puzzled by the strange pain she has felt since meeting Jarvis and Janice together for the first time, until she suddenly understands:

> The long hundred miles did not make her sadder and make her feel more far away than the knowing that they were them and both together and she was only her and parted from them, by herself. And as she sickened with this feeling a thought and an explanation suddenly came to her, so that she knew and almost said aloud: *They are the we of me.*

The expression is utterly characteristic of McCullers: it is grammatically deviant, strikingly peculiar, but – in context – we recognise and understand it as the perfect naming of Frankie's feeling: that Jarvis and Janice together represent something that she, Frankie, in her no-longer-child, not-yet-adult state, is still shut out from, but fervently wants to be part of.

In her desperate belief that Jarvis and Janice will take her with them after the wedding, Frankie (or, as she re-styles herself in her bid to 'belong' to the wedding, F. Jasmine) is, of course, heading for disaster, as Berenice tries to warn her. But even before the events of the wedding day, we see, poignantly and disturbingly, the gap between Frankie's fantasy of her 'belonging', adult self, and her twelve-year-old reality. Dressed up to the nines, on what she believes will be her last day living in her hometown before she goes away with her brother and his bride, Frankie sashays precociously around town and is asked out on a date by a tipsy soldier – who, it becomes clear, takes the five-foot-five Frankie to be much older than she really is. Flattered, yet uneasy, Frankie shows up for the date in the evening, but finds herself adrift in a situation she can only half understand:

> The soldier was both nice and gay, but after he had had two other drinks she wondered if he could be drunk. … To his joking remarks she could never find replies that fitted, although she tried. Like a nightmare pupil in a recital who has to play a duet to a piece she does not know, F. Jasmine did her best to catch the tune and follow. But soon she broke down and grinned until her mouth felt wooden. The blue lights in the crowded room, the smoke and noisy commotion, confused her also.

After a while, the soldier, growing impatient, says, 'Well, Jasmine, how bout going on upstairs?'; and Frankie, still not understanding, but increasingly uneasy, follows him:

> F. Jasmine did not want to go upstairs, but she did not know how to refuse. It was like going into a fair booth, or fair ride, that once having entered you cannot leave… Now it was the same with this soldier, this date. She could not leave until it ended. The soldier was waiting at the foot of the stairs and, unable to refuse, she followed after him… But every footstep F. Jasmine took, she felt somehow was wrong.

When the soldier finally pulls her onto the bed, Frankie bites him, then crashes the heavy water pitcher onto his head and climbs out of the window and down the fire escape, leaving the soldier unconscious on the floor. Thoughts and images she has not previously connected or understood threaten, now, to come together: 'There slanted across her mind twisted remembrances of a common fit in the front room, basement remarks, and nasty Barney; but she did not let these separate glimpses fall together, and the word she repeated was "Crazy" '. Taking refuge in the child-word 'crazy', Frankie veers away from a full realisation or acknowledgment of what has happened; and McCullers foreshadows for us the bitterly inevitable failure of Frankie's attempt, the next day, to become a 'member' of the wedding.

And yet, at the end of the book Frankie – now, properly and femininely, Frances – *does* belong, if not to her brother's wedding, nonetheless to the world it represents: she has a best friend, Mary Littlejohn (who has 'long braids that she could very nearly sit on'); together Frances and Mary make another 'nice white couple', with plans for travelling the world, and scrapbooks, and exaggerated passions (' "I am simply mad about – " But the sentence was left unfinished'). Frankie can move on to take her 'natural' place in society in a way that neither Berenice (eternally excluded as a black woman) nor John Henry (strange, cross-dresssing symbol of childhood) can. But McCullers, at the end of the book, is clearly drawing us back to the kitchen: the child, the girl and the woman, all in their different ways 'unjoined' people, bound together in a strange kind of love through the summer:

> 'But here's this [said Frankie]. I wonder if you have ever thought about this. Here we are – right now. This very minute. Now. But while we're talking right now, this minute is passing. And it will never come again. Never in all the world. When it is gone it is gone. No power on earth could bring it back again. It is gone. Have you ever thought about that?'
>
> Berenice did not answer, and the kitchen was now dark. The three of them sat silent, close together, and they could feel and hear each other's breaths. Then suddenly it started, though why and how they did not know; the three of them began to cry. ... Never before had they suddenly begun to cry; and though their reaons were three different reasons, yet they started at the same instant as though they had agreed together.

McCullers leaves us with an odd, sad feeling of being torn between Frankie's bright, white future, and the 'green and crazy' summer that no power on earth can bring back again.

The Domestic Animal

Jared Diamond, *Guns, Germs and Steel*
(A Short History of Everybody for the Last 13,000 Years)
Vintage, 1998
ISBN 0 09 930278 0

Hugh McAllister

Guns, Germs and Steel is a natural history of human beings. Being about 'us', it contains much to interest a wide range of readers as Diamond sets out to answer the question of a New Guinean: 'Why is it that you white people developed so much cargo and brought it to New Guinea, but we black people had little cargo of our own?' The spread and depth of topics covered is amazing for a single author yet the language is simple and straightforward, and no prior specialist knowledge is required. Whether you have a science PhD or dropped science at the age of sixteen, this book can be easily understood and will give you not only an excellent background to all human history, but also the basic principles of several areas of biology from anthropology and sociology to microbiology and epidemiology.

A unifying theme is the geography of the domestication of plants and animals and the spread of these domesticated forms around the world. It provides an overview, yet also many details, of what is known of the history of the whys and wherefores of the origin of what we call civilisation; why people in certain parts of the world gradually changed from a hunter-gatherer way of life to a settled village and then an urban lifestyle, and why the latter have come to dominate the earth:

> History followed different courses for different peoples because of the differences among peoples' environments, not because of biological differences among peoples themselves.

Anyone looking for arguments to refute claims of the superiority of one human race over another will find them here. You will also find the (curiously Swiftian) reasoning why New Guinea hunter-gatherers may, on average, be more intelligent than the average citizen of the 'developed' world:

> Europeans have for thousands of years been living in densely populated societies with central governments, police, and judiciaries. In these societies, infectious epidemic diseases of dense populations (such as smallpox) were historically the major cause of death [...] Today, most live-born Western infants survive fatal infections as well and reproduce themselves, regardless of their intelligence and the genes they bear. In contrast, New Guineans have been living in societies where human numbers were too low for epidemic diseases of dense populations to evolve. Instead, traditional New Guineans suffered high mortality from murder, chronic tribal warfare, accidents, and problems in procuring food.
>
> Intelligent people are likelier than less intelligent ones to escape these causes of high mortality in traditional New Guinean societies.

This goes to the basis of our understanding of the mechanism of evolution, especially human evolution. The selective forces acting on hunter-gatherers are those which have shaped our evolution over tens of thousands of years until about ten thousand years ago, when 'civilisation' began for most of us. They are very different from the selective forces which act on members of a modern industrial society. Individuals of an egalitarian hunter-gatherer band with little hierarchy and no 'laws' as we understand them who were too aggressive, too 'wimpish', or too stupid, would be less likely to survive, and even less likely to reproduce, than co-operative, intelligent individuals. Are such individuals in our society those who pass most genes on to the next generation? No political point-scoring or political correctness here, just sound biological sense.

The first half of the book deals with the domestication of plants and animals, together with the consequences in terms of the benefits and costs to the people concerned. As far greater populations can be supported by farming than by a hunter-gatherer lifestyle, the farmers, through force of numbers, and usually also the better technology and organisation essential to a settled, farming lifestyle, could easily overwhelm and replace neighbouring hunter-gatherers. Several horrific examples are given of such clashes of cultures, including those between very closely related groups, as with the New Zealand Maoris and the inhabitants of Chatham Island. The meeting of more distantly related cultures accounts for massive genocide. The European colonisation of the Americas led to the loss of probably 95% of native Americans, largely due to disease, though Diamond also gives a graphic account how 168 Spaniards were able to defeat and kill many of an 80,000-strong Inca army.

As with other animal species, co-operation among relatives, but competition, fighting and killing of strangers was the natural behaviour among hunter-gatherer human bands; and this is the state in which humans evolved over hundreds of thousands of years. Many examples are given of how this impulse has continued into ever-larger groupings from tribes to states, and Diamond argues that, following the development of a settled farming lifestyle, it is largely this competition which has led to European dominance. Because its centres of population are isolated from one another by mountains and seas Europe has never been united (the Roman Empire covered only about half of Europe). Any group which did not innovate, or adopt innovations of neighbours, was rapidly conquered or displaced by neighbours who did (genocide is nothing new!). This is contrasted with isolated unified states like China and Japan in which technologies have been abandoned by decree from the ruling oligarchy (ocean-going vessels in medieval China and guns in the samurai period in Japan) despite these countries having the most advanced technologies at the time. These societies survived unconquered for centuries afterwards until globalisation brought them into conflict with societies of European origin. Any European state abandoning such a technology was soon over-run:

> Europe's geographical balkanisation resulted in dozens or hundreds of independent, competing statelets and centres of innovation. If one state did not pursue some particular innovation, another did, forcing neighbouring states to do likewise or else be conquered or left economically behind. Europe's barriers were sufficient to prevent political unification, but insufficient to halt the spread of technology and ideas. There has never been one despot who could turn off the tap for all of Europe, as of China.

Some cultures favour innovation and rapidly adopt new technologies, allowing, encouraging and rewarding individual effort and risk-taking, as with China before about 1450, or Muslim cultures in the medieval period, and the USA (and Europe?) today. In contrast, conservative cultures demanding conformity militate against innovation. Are there lessons to be learnt from this? Perhaps we no longer need to depend on wars for technologically advanced societies to take over the more technologically conservative: globalisation will do the same job. Diamond's examples – the vested interests in gas lighting which greatly delayed the introduction of electric lighting in Britain, and the vested interests in valves which allowed Japan to exploit the American discovery of transistors – should make us wary of the influence of ideological restrictions and commercial vested interests on research and development in current technology.

We talk much today of the potential value to man of the biodiversity of the tropical rainforest and it is true that there may be many useful natural products to be found. On the other hand, Diamond points out that all our major crop and domesticated animal species had been domesticated by Roman times, discussing why so few species are suitable.

> By Roman times almost all of today's leading crops were being cultivated somewhere in the world [...] Ancient hunter-gatherers were intimately familiar with local wild plants, and ancient farmers evidently discovered and domesticated all of those worth domesticating.

There are good reasons why no-one has ridden into battle on a tiger, rhinoceros, or even a zebra, and though elephants have been used since the time of Hannibal, they have never been domesticated, only tamed. The main theme of the book is how the existence of groups of domesticable species in very restricted geographical areas has determined that it is only in these areas that farming could develop. What native Australian or New Zealand plants or animals are cropped for food today? Probably only the Australian macadamia nut (kiwi fruits confusingly are Chinese). The origin and domestication of the most important farmed animals and plants is traced. Many have been changed dramatically from their wild ancestral state due to initially unconscious, and more recently deliberate, selection. Diamond points out that this rapid change under domestication provided Darwin with his strongest arguments and evidence for evolution.

Reading this 'Short History of Everybody' will broaden the mind and knowledge of the scientist and introduce him to the principles of fields other than his own, while for the non-scientist it is an easily intelligible but deep introduction to several biological sciences and the scientific method of reasoning.

Good Books

Have you read any good books recently? Tell us – answers on a postcard – about your all time favourite book, a great book you've read recently or simply the book you're reading at the moment. Many thanks to Dieuwerke Rutgers and Helen Tookey for starting off what we hope will be a popular feature.

Good Books,
The Reader,

Herman Melville, *Moby Dick*

Helen Tookey, *Reader* editor

Reading this book is itself like being swallowed by the Leviathan: you are inside a complete world, one that seems to contain everything: calms and tempests, prose and poetry, cetology and mythology, comedy and tragedy. It also contains some of the most memorable characters you will ever meet: deadpan Ishmael, your guide to all matters touching upon whales; mighty Queequeg, Fiji islander and fearless harpooneer; honest Starbuck, first mate, loyal even though he knows the voyage is doomed; and the compelling Ahab, fatally bound to hunt down his obsession, Moby Dick, the White Whale.

Good Books,
The Reader,
19 Abercromby Square,
Liverpool,
L69 7ZG

Keri Hulme, *The Bone People*

Dieuwerke Rutgers, 22, student

Set in New Zealand, *The Bone People* shows us a world in which two cultures both collide and unite. The unique combination of Maori culture and the Western system of beliefs forces the reader to rethink his or her own identity and surprises us as it reveals the complexity and resilience of human relationships.

Good Books,
The Reader,
19 Abercromby Squa
Liverpool,
L69 7ZG

Reading with Puppy

Sher Schwartz

A puppy has happened to my reading life! Gone are the lengthy reads on the soft brown leather couch and the accompanying enjoyment of steaming tea. I used to extract tasty quotes from whatever I was reading and write them down in my journal. At the same time my journal pages would fill up with comments about characters, questions about the reading, and sometimes – exclamations. All those delightful pastimes are gone.

Here is a ten-week-old puppy. My husband's new hunting dog looks a lot like Han Solo's first mate and co-pilot, Chewbacca. Alibi's Water Ouzel, or Ouzel, as we call her, is a wirehaired pointing griffon – alias Chewie. She has the hairdo, the vocal intonation, and the 'wild gal' archetype honed to a tee. If it wasn't for her smaller size, she could step in as Chewie's stunt back-up.

Now, I'm an off-the-couch reader as Chewie, I mean Ouzel, and I take reading walks. During these outdoor ventures, I steal reading time when and where I can. Except when puppies are sleeping or eating, they always need something, like a romp, to stimulate their overactive nervous systems. Our cabin sits just above the Southeast Alaska high tide line, and every morning, noon, and evening Ouzel and I explore the beach. This morning I'm holding my copy of Bocaccio's *The Decameron* high above puppy-jump line. Below it, equally secure, is Lynne Truss's *Eats, Shoots & Leaves*, and finally my dog-toothed journal, which I've titled *Seen Better Days*.

Ouch!

Ouzel's needle teeth have just penetrated my lightweight jersey pants. I kick her off, bellowing 'Down,' but she lunges back for more. We walk; she lunges, and six high-flies later she spies finer fare – the crashing waves. Her incessant puppy barking at the rollers gives me time to open *The Decameron*. I'm reading the ninth story told on the second day. Zinerva, one of Boccaccio's suggestively modern heroines, has just saved herself from her duped husband's wrath by dressing as a man and gaining the employment and respect of a Sultan. Her deceived husband, who paid 'more attention to another man's falsehoods than to the truth that years of experience should have taught him,' believed the scoundrel Ambrogiuolo's claim that Zinerva has been unfaithful.

Crunch, crunch! Scrape, scrape, scrape.

Ouzel has left the waves and is now chewing on a black rock covered with white barnacles. Jeez, that must hurt.

A glimmering clear and gooey jellyfish has washed ashore; Ouzel notices it, a few feet away, and she drops the rock and lopes toward the Jell-O mass. She stomps and licks it. Next she attacks the rock cress or seaweed strewn along the shore. Each piece is a yellow-brown lobed plant of balloon-like air pockets. Ouzel's needle teeth pop the pockets, producing a hearty *poof* sound. Miss Simple Soft-farts: Ouzel pops one balloon; then another, and she bites and bites in an endless stream of *poof-poofs*. Then jaws fling the deflated rock cress in the air. Through clenched teeth, she swishes the brown flattened plants side to side, as I return to Boccaccio.

Ah, yes. Zinerva still wants her husband, Bernabo, though he commanded her immediate execution; she also wants revenge on the man who made her husband want to kill her. And after years of hiding and hoping, she now has the opportunity to make Ambrogiuolo confess, because both he and her husband are trading in the Sultan's domain. By 'fair means' and 'foul' she arranges for Ambrogiuolo to entertain the Sultan (in front of Bernabo) with the story of how he won five thousand florins unfairly from Bernabo by pretending he had slept with Bernabo's wife Zinerva. By hiding in a chest, Ambrogiuolo was able to see a small mole 'just below her left breast.' This evidence convinced Bernabo his wife had been unfaithful. Once Ambrogioulo has finished bragging about his deed, Zinerva pulls back her manly disguise, tears open her blouse, revealing her breasts, and astounds all three men by proving she is the deceived woman who was supposed to be dead. Her husband, the cad, realizes his error and throws 'himself in tears at her feet.' Ambrogiuolo's luck has just changed, and his next hours will be painful as he's 'tied to the pole and smeared with honey.' Readers will watch while biting insects slowly devour him. The Sultan rewards Zinerva with riches and she happily sails back to Italy with her repentant husband by her side.

Next I open Lynne Truss's recent raucously popular book about punctuation and sit down on the sand. Ouzel climbs a large rock near me and soars off. As she hits the sand her front legs fold under her; her neck extends out like a giraffe; her head goes kerplunk, and her brown ears stretch out across the shore. She's suspended, tied for a moment to the dune; then, she's up racing back and forth across the beach.

I pick up where I recently left off reading on page 118 about the 'annunciatory' colon:

> This much is clear, Watson: it was the baying of an enormous hound.

Crash! The page has disappeared; Ouzel explodes into my lap; a muddy paw print threatens to blot out 'Watson: it was the baying of an enormous hound.' If Lynne Truss were here she would see – woman reading: puppy coming.

No!

That's it; I give up; I've lost the books beneath a huge amount of Chewie-like brown hair. I sit on the books. Truss's American white-covered edition is now buried in the sand. *Seen Better Days*'s pages are torn, and *The Decameron*, suddenly, seems extremely well read. The puppy has slid off me, and she's lying on her back. Recall someone, a child perhaps, playing air-guitar; Ouzel is playing running-air. Her legs paw frantically; she bites at the sky and me, if she can get me; she groans (a bizarre puppy-thing), and I – with nothing else to do – begin to sing. It must be my child-side replacing the restrained academic, for I croon 'Are your big teeth coming in, your little teeth aren't a friend; when will your big teeth come in?' We buzz like this; she groans and howls on her back with all four legs sticking straight up, and I sing, sing, for a time. Then she rolls over and is off running, and another 'reading walk' is closed. There's always the lunch break to look forward to; maybe I can finish *Eats, Shoots & Leaves* then?

I may dream of the leather couch, the hot tea, the long sighs over a beautiful literary passage, but for a few months, anyway, it'll be me and the puppy trying to get in a little reading when and where we can.

EnCompass Reading

Susan Tranter

When I tell people I'm a Reader in Residence for a website, they usually give me what can politely be referred to as a quizzical look. What *is* a Reader in Residence, exactly, and how can you be 'in residence' on a website?

It makes more sense when I explain the nature of the website: the British Council's EnCompass Culture site (www.encompass-culture.com), a kind of international online book resource, which provides loads of information about UK and Commonwealth writing, selected book lists, tips on starting reading groups, and so on. The name refers to the way the 5,000+ books on the website's database are organised: readers can choose points from around a spinning on-screen 'compass' to refine a personal search for books they might like. There are separate compasses for adults, teenagers and children, and within each one the points refer to different genres (fiction, poetry, travel, biography, science, and crime fiction, among others, on the adult compass; with many helpful sub-categories once you've selected one of those).

The trouble with websites, of course, is that you need to find a way of keeping the information they contain fresh, and making the site look different and interesting each time people visit it, which is where I come in. My job is to write reviews of some of those 5,000-odd titles, make a 'Book of the Month' recommendation, write a regular newsy column, create readers' quizzes on different topics or genres, facilitate author interviews (where visitors to the site ask the questions by emailing them in), and look after the discussion boards where readers from around the world discuss topics ranging from 'my favourite place to read' (for the under 12s) to the relative merits of film adaptations of books.

If I've managed thus far to hold the attention of whoever I'm explaining all this to, they usually agree by this point that it's a pretty good job to have. Which is true because central to it all is reading. I read, I would say, around four books a month from the EnCompass lists in order to keep up to date and create those reviews and recommendations. If I'm going to be interviewing a writer, I'll want to make sure I've read their books. And if there's an online discussion about a writer or a book, I don't want to look a fool by having to ask an elementary question because I haven't read the work involved.

Reading books for a living can't be bad. I often find myself stretched out on the sofa with a cup of tea, engrossed in a book, and can't help thinking: 'I'm *working*. While everyone else is rushing for the office, answering the phone or dealing with angry customers, I'm doing this.' It's inevitable though that I've brought to the job my own tastes and predispositions for certain kinds of writing, or even certain kinds of writers. My 'Books of the Month' are usually novels, for instance. And I know I tend to lean towards what's usually referred to as 'literary fiction'. The roll-call of my recommended titles from the last six months reads: David Mitchell, Jeanette Winterson, Ian McEwan, James Kelman, Jhumpa Lahiri and Hari Kunzru – arguably a fairly narrow range. But at the same time my work on EnCompass – rather like attending a reading group, which I do in Manchester – has brought about some fortuitous discoveries, and encouraged me to read things I would never even have picked up in a library or a bookshop. For instance, I knew precious little about African writing before I was asked to help run some on-line chats between readers in the UK and Africa which had been set up by the British Council as part of its Africa@21 project. I scurried off to the library and came back with an armful of books, one of which was Chinua Achebe's *Things Fall Apart*, a title familiar to me from my A-level days, when a teacher had enthusiastically encouraged me to read it (though somehow I never had). It turned out my teacher was right: it *is* a fantastic novel – totally different to anything I've read before, infused with a gravity and a dignity and a real elegance all its own.

I'd be fibbing though if I didn't say that the blessings are mixed sometimes. For every great find or satisfying discovery there's a book which confirms my prejudices against it ('now I know why I walked straight past it in the library all those times'). I'm not going to name names, of course. But don't we all know the experience of reading a book and feeling afterwards that our time has been wasted? Perhaps I'm more of a snob than I would like to admit, but I do feel there's not enough time to read all the great books, let alone all the less-than-greats.

The best part of my work is undoubtedly when someone emails me to say that they've just read a book on my recommendation – perhaps by an author they'd never felt like trying before – and really enjoyed it. This happened with Zoë Heller's *Notes on a Scandal*, and more recently with David Mitchell's *Cloud Atlas* (a book I invariably start trying to plug to people in a sentence or two, but end up raving about for at least twenty minutes). A few months back someone dropped me a line to say they were going to try James Kelman's *Translated Accounts* after reading my Book of the Month recommendation: they weren't even put off by the warning that it's a book without any real plot, an unknown setting and no defined characters. All of this is great, and it's one way in which online reviewing surpasses newspaper or magazine work: most critics publishing in print rarely find out if anyone reads their opinions, let alone if anyone acts on them.

I should say that this isn't the only work I do, so the reading I do for EnCompass isn't my only reading. I take an almost guilty pleasure in reading something which *doesn't* fall within EnCompass territory – in practice this usually means work by writers from beyond the UK / Commonwealth boundary. I like a lot of contemporary writing from the United States; I've a weakness for the crazy world of Japanese novelist Haruki Murakami; and I like to try European work in translation too. My New Year's reading resolution this year was to read more non-fiction. I *must* increase my intake of biography, travel, general mind-expanding writing…

When I was studying English at university, I'd sometimes sigh at the pile of texts I was wading through, and long for the day when I could read what I liked, be it high-brow or gutter-trash. Now I find that having that freedom is great, but sometimes we miss the guidance that a structured reading list can bring – one of the reasons, perhaps, for the popularity of reading groups today. My involvement in the EnCompass website fulfils that kind of 'guiding' role for me (as I hope it does also for people who use the site), and when my tenure as Reader in Residence comes to an end, I suspect I'll miss it a good deal.

As for myself,
Where first I met the bitter scent is lost.
I, too, often shrivel the grey shreds,
Sniff them and think and sniff again and try
Once more to think what it is I am remembering,
Always in vain.
(Edward Thomas, from 'Old Man')

subscribe

Make sure of your copy of *The Reader*
and enjoy big savings*
by taking out a **subscription**:

UK

1 year	4 issues	**£18.00**
2 years	8 issues	**£30.00**
3 years	12 issues	**£38.00**

US**

1 year	4 issues	**$30.00**
2 years	8 issues	**$50.00**
3 years	12 issues	**$65.00**

Elsewhere

1 year	4 issues	**£24.00**
2 years	8 issues	**£46.00**
3 years	12 issues	**£62.00**

Please make cheques payable to the University of Liverpool and post to **The Reader, 19 Abercromby Square, University of Liverpool, L69 7ZG**.

Include your name and address and specify the issue with which you would like your subscription to begin.

* Actual cover price £6.00
** The easiest way to take out a US subscription is using Paypal on our website: www.thereader.co.uk

Newman's Notes

A Word for Jane Austen (1)

The first of an occasional series in which good friend of The Reader *Stephen Newman posthumously shares unfailingly vivid insights on a wide range of subjects, both literary and otherwise.*

Stephen Newman

Let me begin with the obvious, the words on the page. Take the most famous opening gambit in world literature, 'It is a truth universally acknowledged, that a single man in possession of a large fortune must be in want of a wife.'

How shall we read this? It is as cheeky as a Wilde epigram, as weighty as a Euclid axiom and as bafflingly various as a Rubik's cube. The more you read it the more you realise it is not so much prose as a whizzing field of force. The only artist I can think of who creates a like expectancy and richness out of such elementary – and elemental – material is Beethoven. In a flash a universe is revealed.

It is a style instinct with wit, and wit is a dangerous property: mercurial, irreverent, explosive, visionary, anarchic. 'Man of wit, bad character', wrote Pascal. Unless harnessed to understanding it is as self- and socially-destructive as a hand grenade. As Mr Darcy says, 'The wisest and best of men, nay, the wisest and best of their actions, may be rendered ridiculous by a person whose first object in life is a joke' – a solid pudding of a rebuke which is set on fire by the brandy of Elizabeth Bennet's badinage. Jane Austen was aware of this battle between wit and sense. in a letter she wrote, 'Wisdom is better than Wit, & in the long run will certainly have the laugh on her side' – a statement that confirms the essentially comic thrust of her genius. But it is also another germ-cell, illuminating the essentially dramatic quality of her art.

'Dramatise, dramatise,' wrote Henry James. Jane Austen is

all drama. Take the great scene in chapter 15 of *Mansfield Park* where Fanny is embroiled in the theatricals. Almost every sentence quivers with meaning and counter-meaning, from Fanny's pregnant cry, 'No, indeed, I cannot act', to Mary Crawford's kindness which paradoxically restores her to 'all the little she had lost in Edmund's favour', while the texture flashes between Mr Rushworth's farcical cry, 'If you are afraid of half a dozen speeches… what would you do with such a part as mine? I have forty-two to learn', and Mrs Norris's unforgiveable outburst 'very ungrateful indeed, considering who and what she is' (no writer except Shakespeare captures more the chameleon-like colours of individual idiolects). The sum of the drama is that the social cage in which Fanny is imprisoned shakes as though a great white shark were attacking it. Fanny's devotion is at once exposed by this battery and concealed by it. One of the fundamental laws of love – loneliness – is almost brutally revealed.

Mansfield Park alerts us to the peculiar, enduring, unassuageable central theme of Jane Austen – love. Either her characters know they are in love but are unable to act, like Fanny Price and Anne Elliot, or they don't realise they are in love, like Elizabeth Bennet and Emma. In the latter there is a void which all her plots and machinations serve only to highlight.

The great Box Hill scene in chapter 43 is the crisis. Again, it is to music that you turn for analogy – to the minuet in *Don Giovanni* against which the Don makes his attempt upon Zerlina. There is the same courtly formality which builds and builds until atmosphere crackles. The social badinage positively screams with banality until the storm breaks and Emma finds 'the tears running down her cheeks almost all the way home, without being at any trouble to check them, extraordinary as they were'.

> Some simple things take a long time to get thought out.
>
> (Bernard Malamud, from *Dubin's Lives*)

Our Spy in NY

Enid Stubin

At the end of an infernal summer in the city, when even stoic New Yorkers whimpered about the oppressive heat, I found myself at a table for six at an East Village trattoria for a friend's birthday. Seated in the verdant back garden were Pandora, a filmmaker; her husband Carmen, a painter; Revina, an actress and model; and Gwen, the birthday celebrant, who also models and writes and acts in films. We all knew Gwen, but few of us knew each other, and so once introductions were made, conversation came tumbling out. For the two of us who teach for a living, Pandora posed a question: 'Who's your idea of a fake writer?' Without explanation or qualification, Gwen answered: 'Joyce Carol Oates. She writes the same damn book every other year.' That observation struck me as trenchant. As an undergraduate I'd marveled at the stories in *The Wheel of Love* and then watched every plot and theme in them mined for this novel, that short story, or an independent film over the next three decades.

Some years ago I was copy-editing a respected fiction magazine, where I made a point of dealing with the manuscripts written by graduate students, independent authors, and a few literary hotshots, as gently and unobtrusively as possible. After all, I served as copy and not acquisitions editor; by the time a text reached my chaotic desktop, it had already been accepted for publication. My job, as I saw it, was to edit as gingerly as possible in order to preserve the author's voice. But when it came to Oates's submission, a sprawling, forty-page account of a sadistic sorority hazing at an Ivy League college, something snapped halfway through and I – there's no other word for it – slashed my way through the Courier font typescript, excising incantatory refrains, querying solecisms, and cutting the story by a third. I'd not done anything comparable in twenty years of freelance editing and was preparing some heapish apology for my presumption and tumescent red pencil to the editor and publisher, who called and said that Oates was 'thrilled – she wished she'd had you for an editor years earlier.' Go figure: even Oates herself could see it. And now, on a late-summer's evening in Lower Manhattan, the truth was revealed. And not by me, but by three of the most beautiful and talented women in New York, actors, dancers, and filmmakers who filled the air not with talk of auditions and grants, bookings and agents and film festivals, but with talk of books and their importance in the world.

This was fun. Who else was a fake writer? 'Camille Paglia.' Oh, yes – The Reluctant Academic Debutante. How I'd quarreled with friends who bought *Sexual Personae* for its title or even, lord love 'em, to read: 'It's awful, and no, I can't quite say why.' But the readers at our table knew why: because she's a fake writer. Not a merely bad writer: Barbara Cartland, Danielle Steele, and James Clavell write engaging trash that never sets itself up as more than that. But fake writers suck up all the air in the room, not to mention pages in the arts sections. Emerging or even established writers can never hope to meet their output, their reviews, their omnipresence in the newspapers and literary journals.

Last night the novelist John Irving showed up on *The Daily Show*, a wicked parody of television news programs that sends up the bite-sized reports, shallow 'in-depth' analysis, and mechanical interviews that serve to promote whatever project – movie, television series, tell-all autobiography, nutritional bible – some celebrity has on his or her plate. Witless but blandly affable, Irving rambled through an anecdote about his mentor, Kurt Vonnegut, Jr., that had clearly been rehearsed. More revealing was the discussion of narrative technique with Jon Stewart, the impish host of the show, which suggested Irving's fictional templates. Even during the more heated and improbable of Irving's sex scenes, Stewart noted, 'There's always a bear on roller skates in the background.' Irving laughed ruefully but had the grace to shrug in acquiescence. Well, he'd have to, wouldn't he? He's a fake writer.

That evening at I Coppi, I not only understood but experienced 'On Inviting a Friend to Supper.' Exchanges in two languages and several dialects sparkled in the candlelight; the chef, Maristella, recommended risotto ai funghi; Pandora whispered 'You know, Florentines are usually very stuck-up, but she isn't'; and I felt immersed in the glamour of the Jonsonian dinner party, surrounded by sophisticated, articulate, funny, and discerning artists, performers, and teachers eager to discuss books and the place of the intellectual in American life. 'What about Edmund Wilson?' Carmen demanded in mock belligerence. 'What's so great about him?' I understood Carmen's resistance. Having come to read Wilson late in life (as I refer to my graduate school years), I had trouble making sense of the zigzagging trajectory of his political passions, his wildly far-flung aesthetic preoccupations, including his preference for Minsky's strippers, zaftig and reliably ethnic as opposed to the long-legged Nordic types featured at the Ziegfeld Follies. And pleased to be remembering all these arcana over good food and wine, I turned to the professor of Romantic literature at the table and said in attribution, 'Richard Locke introduced me to Edmund Wilson.' Usually too kind and courtly to catch me up in a name-dropping gaffe, he countered, 'Judith Rascoe introduced me to Edmund Wilson.' Of course, I was talking about paperback reprints assigned for a survey course taught by an urbane editor at the *New York Times Book Review* and *Vanity Fair*, while Larry had actually spent the day with Wilson and his wife Elena at their summer home in Wellfleet, Massachusetts, through the offices of a Harvard classmate. But the story suggests why Wilson is important, both as essayist and as literary cynosure – someone who spent as much time living as writing – and so it answered Carmen's question even as it revealed my own klutziness in the matter of reception theory, otherwise known as literary gossip.

What else about the charm of that evening? The fact that a single pair of reading glasses – they happened to be mine – circulated the table for purposes of reading the menu and wine list? That homey detail proved yet another point of commonality among us. Performing artists and writers traditionally have seen themselves as avowed rivals, competitors for funding, prestige, and the hearts and minds of the populace, and guess who appears to have won in a walk? The idea that people in the arts are thinking about the role of the writer in contemporary society is plenty compelling. Now if the literati could relax about the glittering prizes and come to the table, they too might find 'the entertaynment perfect' – the engagement, the generosity, and the odd dialect joke along with the Carmignano and the rack of lamb and the liberty that we enjoyed that night.

> Now I know that Spring will come again,
> Perhaps to-morrow: however late I've patience
> After this night following on such a day.
>
> (Edward Thomas, from 'March')

Ask the Reader

Q The countryside has changed so much in the last fifty years that the most casual references to it in older literature are now incomprehensible. 'Fair daffodils we weep to see / You haste away so soon' becomes absurd as a response to the wilting flowers bought from the supermarket when Herrick was thinking of the Lent lily, the wild-flower, which, as my handbook says, is 'absent as native from large areas'. What connection can our minds make with his?

A Feelings don't date though their occasions may; Herrick grieves for the brevity of our joys of which the flowering of a *Narcissus pseudonarcissus* is just one. Spring is poignant because the winter cold is over yet our pleasure at its return is forgotten in its normality. The fate of the daffodil is also ours; 'We have short time to stay as you, / We have as short a spring', a middle-aged regret for lost youth with its grace and sense of a brave new world. 'Well, I know that,' I hear you reply, 'But the image diverts attention away from the subject to what the Devon countryside looked like in the 1630s. The poem for me is tourism, like Devon is for most people today.' Yes, 'Houston, we have a problem'. When even the seasons cease to affect us deeply something has fundamentally changed. In January, we travel from centrally-heated rooms in heated cars to heated shops, offices and factories, so winter is only a mild inconvenience. Supplies of food and light scarcely vary throughout the year. We have hankerings, of course, so we feed the birds with Bill Oddie, cultivate the garden with Monty Don, keep domestic animals and watch wild things on TV, but natural process has little place in our consciousness except as anxiety about climate change. In *News from Nowhere* William Morris imagines a visitor from the 1830s to a future in which farming has become central again and remembers his own times when the intelligentsia had 'a kind of sour distaste for the changing drama of the year, for the life of earth and its dealings with men'. For us, nature's 'dealings' shock with the destructive power of hurricanes and tsunamis. Instead of a habitual presence, nature becomes an occasional disaster reminding us of our neglect and the frailty and insignificance of our self-created habitats.

But there are qualifications of this apparent change in our consciousness. If we have such intimations of the inexorability of forces beyond our control, then we do share in Herrick's lament for the transience of his daffodils. When we express such fears we often use the same images. Personally I have a regret for the passing of the old cheerful Morris Minor, closer to a beetle than even the classic VW, but a poem that wept for its loss might amuse, awaken memory, be politically acute about the wasting of resources, but would not touch even a townie like me so much as Herrick's flowers. Their ephemerality and beauty is a constant whether in a Devon lane in 1635 or the shelves of your local Tesco. When the Bible prefers the splendour of lilies to the glory of Solomon, it really does not matter if the image that flashes on your mental screen owes more to the florist's shop than to historical accuracy. It is the prodigality of natural beauty that we witness.

Nor is it purely at the level of emotions that Herrick's image survives. Natural things in our man-made world where everything has a measured cause and consequence constitute, to use a trendy term, the other, the unpredictable, the simply there, a kind of truth. As such we think of them, unscientifically no doubt, as belonging together. Daffodils and stars belong in a single category in so far as we see in them the non-human, the unmade, and that is clearer to us in our cluttered world than even it was for Herrick. As such, in a non-religious time, we tend to invest their presence with a kind of diversity as all belonging to the uncontrollable, invested with the attributes of permanence. Thought and idea are stimulated by such images because in the end we are more like daffodils than Morris Minors; we die but we are not superseded. The term 'natural' continues to have meaning for us because we are in it and it is in us.

> The Past is a strange land, most strange.
> Wind blows not there, nor does rain fall:
> If they do, they cannot hurt at all.
> Men of all kinds as equals range
>
> The soundless fields and streets of it.
> (Edward Thomas, from 'Parting')

Dear Editor,

I was delighted to see an issue of *The Reader* devoted to The Sea, but disappointed that room could not be found for a discussion of James Hanley. I believe he is one of the twentieth century's most neglected authors, and, though he was born in Dublin, he was brought up in Liverpool, and spent much of his adult life in North Wales, so there is an added reason for commemorating him in your pages.

Hanley's contribution to sea literature is different from that of most other writers on the subject. Apart from being a compulsive and prolific author he also presented a working-class perspective. He went to sea when he was in his early teens and his experience as a deck-hand informed much of his creative output. *Boy* told the truth about the exploitation, both psychological and sexual, that went on aboard cargo-ships, and was banned for many years. His identification with proletarian values gave his accounts a terrible authenticity. But he possessed the true writer's empathy to a high degree, and in *The Closed Harbour* he portrayed the life of a ship's captain in a narrative as sophisticated as the best of Conrad. In *The Ocean* at times he approached the symbolic power of Melville.

Since Hanley also wrote some of the finest fiction that has come out of rural North Wales – most notably in *Anatomy of Llangwyllych, The Welsh Sonata* and *The Kingdom* – I hope you will see fit to publish a feature on him in the future.

John Killick

Dear Editor,

I found the extract from John Carey's new book, *What Good are the Arts?* printed in *Reader* 19 very stimulating. His balanced approach to the familiar topic of juvenile delinquency is refreshing: he neither sympathises nor condemns; instead, he explains. It makes sense to me that literature should provide readers with an opportunity to discover and articulate problems in their own lives. Reading is a controlled and safe escape, but it does not enjoy the 'cool' status of drugs and drink (those uncontrolled and risky escapes) because of the jarring of two social expectations, i.e. children must learn to read (society says) but they must also hate to do it once they can (their peers affirm). I could go on and on about Carey's new book because it is itself a perfect example of the kind of work it praises: *What Good are the Arts?* 'develops and enlarges the mind as well as changing it.'

Eileen Pollard

The Reader Crossword

Cassandra No.12

Across

9. Slight tremor on Italian volcanic island causes sensation of pelvic pain (9)

10. Instrument to suppress little woman (5)

***11 and 20 across.** Can we contrive for apostle to represent our heroine? (5, 5)

12. Not free to obtain limited tenure (9)

13. Given aid a craft centre will turn round a traditional rural area (7)

14. Iago's old occupation (7)

17. Part of topic ultimately up for discussion is concerned with weight of Asian people (5)

***19.** See 24 down

***20.** See 11 across

***21.** See 8 down

***22.** See 4 down

24. Reprobate in a band on Edinburgh stage (9)

26. First of all lots of old friends are cool and distant (5)

28. African perhaps reversing in major general's car (5)

29. Less accomplished winter sportsman finds himself outside alien church (9)

* Clues with an asterisk have a common theme

Down

1. Payment for services rendered is beginning of fortune in Essex families (4)

2. Free choice nonetheless contains what sounds like imitation (6)

3. Luigi has six characters looking for him and one lord circling in plane (10)

***4 and 22 across.** Swift's journal belonging to Roman historian reveals our author (6,7)

5. This Irish son of the sea leads the band (8)

6. Sounds as if the first murder victim is competent (4)

7. Often unwanted entrants (8)

***8, 21 across and 27 down.** Lack of warmth at McDonalds, the setting for our story (4, 7, 4)

13. Does Nora's picnic include jelly? (5)

15. Can a cap and alb transform this Grand Master from Cuba? (10)

16. This lock cannot be picked (5)

18. Disturb a camping expedition (8)

19. Surprise means Ashton is in turmoil (8)

22. Glad to lose a pound with apparent gush of water from this device (6)

23. Seems like a breath of fresh air in a performance of the Wizard of Oz on ice (6)

***24, 19 across and 25 down.** Someone who saw something nasty when member of family and palindromic girl have a change of mood (4, 3, 4)

***25.** See 24 down

***27.** See 8 down

Buck's Quiz 20
Love Us, Love our Dogs

1. Whose poem retells the story of a prince's faithful hound who kills a wolf to save his master's baby son but the prince, thinking the dog has slain the baby, kills the dog before finding the baby alive and well?
2. What is the name of William Brown's dog?
3. Whose son was shot by a farmer after driving a flock of sheep over a precipice?
4. Where did Mark Haddon find the title for his best-selling novel?
5. How does the Prioress in Chaucer's *Canterbury Tales* feed her dogs?
6. What is the name of the dog given to Florence who was 'continually acting on a wrong idea that there was an enemy in the neighbourhood, whom it was meritorious to bark at'?
7. In which novel does Throttler, a half-breed bulldog and the son of Skulker, appear?
8. Which dog recognised his master after his return from war and died from joy?
9. Which single parent shoots a rabid dog, much to the surprise of his children?
10. Which dog was stolen from his master, Judge Miller, and taken to the Arctic?
11. In which novel, set against the fall of the Berlin Wall, do Communist Party members June and Bernard meet and fall in love?
12. Which novelist painted a picture of her family's pet dog Keeper taking a nap?
13. Which eponymous heroine tries to rescue a little rough terrier named Snap?
14. Who said 'I think Crab my dog be the sourest-natured dog that lives'?
15. Who left the graveyard every day at the one o'clock gun for his mid-day meal?
16. Who lodged this objection to a trip: 'Scenery is not my line and I don't smoke. If I see a rat, you won't stop and if I go to sleep, you get fooling about with the boat and slop me overboard'?
17. Which story includes Bob, Gypsy, Pirate, Postboy, Stumpy, Tipkins and Timothy Gyp?
18. In which book does Hagrid's boarhound Fang first appear?
19. Which author took his pet poodle Charlie on a 10,000 mile journey round America?
20. What was the name of Walter Scott's black greyhound?

Contributors 20

Neil Curry's study of the eighteenth-century poet Christopher Smart was published earlier this year. His most recent collection of poems is *The Road to the Gunpowder House* (Enitharmon Press).
Gabriella Gruder-Poni is a teacher living in New York City.
Jen Hadfield is a poet and photographer whose first collection, *Almanacs*, was published by Bloodaxe this year. Her website is http://www.rogueseeds.co.uk.
Alexander Heald lives and works in London, where he was born. He is married.
John Kinsella's most recent volumes are *Peripheral Light: Selected and New Poems* (W.W. Norton, 2003), *Doppler Effect: Collected Experimental Poems* (Salt, 2004), and *The New Arcadia* (W.W. Norton, 2005). He is a Fellow of Churchill College, Cambridge.
Pamela Lewis' series of poems written to mark the 1985 D.H. Lawrence celebrations, *Cycle for a Centenary*, is to be made accessible in the context of the Lawrence web resources on the University of Nottingham website.
Hugh McAllister was the botanist at the University of Liverpool Botanic Gardens at Ness from 1972 until being transferred to the School of Biological Sciences in 1997.
Michael Murphy's *Elsewhere* is published by Shoestring Press. He lectures in English Literature at Liverpool Hope University, and is currently writing a book about Marcel Proust's American influences.
Les Murray. Oz poet Les Murray once wrote: The true God gives his flesh and blood: idols demand yours off you.
Adam Piette is Professor at the University of Sheffield, author of *Remembering and the Sound of Words* and *Imagination at War*.
Ralph Pite teaches English at the University of Liverpool. His biography of Thomas Hardy will be published by Picador in spring 2006.
Jacob Polley's first book of poems, *The Brink*, was published by Picador in 2003. He has recently been appointed Fellow Commoner in the Arts at Trinity College, Cambridge, 2005–2007.
Jane Routh manages woodlands and a flock of geese in North Lancashire. Her *Circumnavigation* won the Poetry Business Competition 2002 and was shortlisted for the Forward (Best First Collection)

Prize.

Chris Routledge is a freelance writer and editor who specialises in American literature, history, and biography. He is co-editor of *Key Thinkers in Linguistics* and *The Philosophy of Language*, Edinburgh 2005.

Sher Schwartz lives in Ketchikan, Alaska with her homing pigeons, ducks, cats, dog, and husband. She teaches Interdisciplinary Humanities and English for the University of Alaska.

Vicky Seal is a writer and editor interested in the healing and mysticism of the New Age. Along the way she has spent years caring for special-needs tortoises.

Ann Stapleton is a freelance writer from Ohio whose work has appeared or is forthcoming in *Alaska Quarterly Review, The Dark Horse*, and *The Weekly Standard.*

Enid Stubin is Assistant Professor of English at Kingsborough Community College of the City University of New York and Adjunct Professor of Humanities at New York University's School of Continuing and Professional Studies.

Linda Taylor is currently working as a Management Accountant in UoL Finance Office. She has an MA in Victorian Literature from The University of Liverpool.

Matt Thomas is an assistant and regional ranger for Wirral Country Park.

Susan Tranter works on projects involving books and publishers. She is co-Chair of the National Association for Literature Development, and lives in Manchester.

Mary Weston was born in Hawaii and now lives in Liverpool. She is a facilitator for the community-based project Get Into Reading. Her novel *The Escape Plan* was published in 2001.

Buck's Quiz 19

1.Walden **2.** *Let Us Now Praise Famous Men*, James Agee **3.** Edna St Vincent Millay **4.** F. Scott Fitzgerald **5.** *As I Lay Dying* **6.** Wendell Berry **7.** Henry James, *Portrait of a Lady* **8.** H.D **9.** Raymond Chandler **10.** Emily Dickinson **11.** Gertrude Stein **12.** Flannery O'Connor **13.** *Fences*, August Wilson **14.** *Mourning Becomes Electra* **15.** *Death of a Salesman* **16.** Larry McMurty **17.** Damon Runyon **18.** *The Moon is Down*, J.Steinbeck **19.** *Native Son* **20.** *Herzog*

Prizes! Please send your answers to Buck's Quiz, The Reader, 19 Abercromby Square, Liverpool L69 7ZG

Cassandra Crossword 11

Across

1. Oleograph **6.** Wrath **9.** The Aspern Papers **10.** Eats **11.** Myrmidon **14.** Diarrhoea **15.** India **16.** Wings **18.** Reediness **20.** Pastimes **21.** Knew **25.** Portrait of a Lady **26.** Sumps **27.** Exerciser

Down

1. Of the **2.** Electra **3.** Gist **4.** Amen **5.** Henry James **6.** What Maisie **7.** Amended **8.** Hosannahs **12.** Brassieres **13.** Bourgeoise **14.** Downpipes **17.** Nostrum **19.** Enneads **22.** Wryer **23.** Dove **24.** Talc

Distribution Information

For trade orders in all territories except North America and Mexico, please contact:
Marston Book Services, PO Box 269, Abingdon, OX14 4YN, UK
Tel: +44 [0]1235 465 500 **Fax:** +44 [0]1235 465 555
Email: trade.order@marston.co.uk **Web:** www.marston.co.uk

For trade orders in North America and Mexico, please contact:
University of Chicago Press, 1427 East 60th Street, Chicago, Illinois 60637, USA
Tel: +1 800 621 2736 **Fax:** +1 800 621 8476
Email: custserv@press.uchicago.edu **Web:** www.press.uchicago.edu

For institutional subscriptions in all territories, please contact:
Sarah Preece, Subscriptions, Marston Book Services Ltd,
PO Box 269, Abingdon, Oxfordshire, OX14 4YN, UK
Tel: +44 [0]1235 465 537 **Email:** subscriptions@marston.co.uk

If you have any queries regarding trade orders or institutional subscriptions, please contact Janet Smith at Liverpool University Press on +44 [0]151 794 2233 or email janmar@liv.ac.uk